BATH PORTRAIT

Books by Bryan Little

BATHS MUSEUM; MINERVA HEAD

BATH PORTRAIT

The Story of Bath, its Life and its Buildings

by

BRYAN LITTLE

THE BURLEIGH PRESS
BRISTOL
1980

© BRYAN LITTLE

I.S.B.N. 0 902780 06 9

First Published 1961
Second Edition 1968
Third Edition 1972
Fourth Edition 1980

MADE AND PRINTED IN GREAT BRITAIN BY
BURLEIGH LIMITED AT THE BURLEIGH PRESS
BRISTOL

CONTENTS

LIST OF ILLUSTRATIONS

FOREWORD

FOR this fourth edition of a book which still, in Bath and elsewhere, meets a genuine demand I have left the text of the first nine chapters unchanged, but have much revised, and largely rewritten, the final chapter on "More Recent Times". I have thus been able to take account of events and new buildings since 1972, and still more of the great wave of renovation, cleaning, and conservation which, in Bath as in its larger neighbour Bristol, has transformed many of the city's historic buildings. Restoration and renovation has, indeed, been on a spectacular scale, and in the most historic and most visited parts of Bath it is, for financial and other reasons, much more important than the construction of wholly new buildings. There are, however, strong prospects of a supermarket near the station, first called Queen Square and more recently Green Park, built by the Midland Railway over a hundred years ago, while new Law Courts, originally planned for the empty space near the Beaufort Hotel, now seem a real possibility at the junction of Milk and James Streets. This building will be a responsibility of Avon County. I hope that it will, without slavery to neo-Georgianism, be of a good contemporary design.

My links with Bath, a city I have now known well for over thirty-five years, have remained close in various ways, particularly from my position as the architectural correspondent of the *Bath and West Evening Chronicle*. Many of my descriptive points, and my comments on recent work, have been drawn from articles, of appreciation and criticism, which I have written for that newspaper.

B.D.G.L.
Bristol, February, 1980.

ix

ACKNOWLEDGMENTS

Among those to whom my thanks are due for their kind help during the writing and revision of this book I wish to mention the late Town Clerk of Bath (Mr. Jared E. Dixon) and his successor, Mr. N. J. L. Pearce, LL.M.; Mr. Peter Pagan, B.A., F.L.A. (Director of the Victoria Art Gallery and Municipal Libraries); Miss C. M. L. Munday, F.L.A., and members of the staff of the Bath Municipal Libraries; Miss D. M. Bushell and Mr. Michael Owen, late Curators of the Roman Baths Museum; the late City Planning Officer (Mr. J. G. Wilkinson, A.R.I.B.A.); Dr. R. E. Stutchbury and Mr. Roy Worskett, both previously City Architects and Planning Officers, and Mr. K. J. Cotton, Mr. J. G. Ruddick and Mr. B. Barry of the City Planning Office; Mr. Ernest Tew, F.R.I.B.A.; Mr. I. P. Collis, M.A. (lately Somerset County Archivist) and members of his staff at Taunton; Mr. J. G. Yardley, O.B.E. past Secretary of the Bath and West and Southern Counties Society; and Mr. G. M. Yates, Clerk to the Bristol Avon River Authority, and Mr. G. Denbury, Public Relations Officer, University of Bath.

B.D.G.L.

ACKNOWLEDGMENTS FOR ILLUSTRATIONS

By courtesy of Spa Department, Bath Corporation:—Frontispiece, plates 1, 2.
By courtesy, Mr. T. W. Snailum, F.R.I. B.A. :—plate 47.
By courtesy, National Monuments Record :—plates 18, 21, 22, 23, 24, 29, 35, 37, 40.
Photographs, Reece Winstone :—plates 4, 12, 16, 33, 36.
Photographs, W. A. Morris :—plates 3, 5, 6, 7, 9, 10, 11, 13, 15, 19, 20, 26, 27, 28, 30, 31, 32, 34, 38, 39, 41, 43, 44, 45, 46, 48, 51, 52.
Photographs, Bath & West Evening Chronicle:—plates 14, 25, 28.
Photograph, University of Bath:—plate 49.
By courtesy, King Edward VI Grammar School:—plate 8.
By courtesy, Hugh Roberts, Graham and Stollar:—plates 41, 51.
By courtesy, Herman Miller Company:—plate 50.

Chapter I

FIRST FLOWERING

LET us first retrace the steps of Jane Austen's Catherine Morland, climbing steeply up the path along the edge of Beechen Cliff whose lofty, wooded precipice so boldly overhung the southern extremity of Bath. A few gaps in the trees give us splendid vantage points for an aerial survey, and this hill has always been perfectly placed for overlooking the city's site. In the 1790's, when Jane Austen wrote "Northanger Abbey", the district was less densely built over than it is to-day. At the foot of Beechen Cliff, and in the whole suburb of Lyncombe–Widcombe, many houses had yet to arise when Catherine and her friends gazed over the scene. In the main city, Georgian terraces and other formal groupings were more evident than in the more sprawling, haphazard modern Bath. The landscape was not without its hilly or wooded elements of "picturesqueness", but was less obviously "romantic" than the grander scenery of the Welsh Marches or the Gorge at Clifton. So in Catherine's starry eyes the somewhat formal Bath scene could be set aside as "unworthy to make part of a landscape". But it may yet content the gaze of those less insistent than Miss Morland on the essentials of "The Picturesque". What we must also consider is how the site of Bath, uncumbered with its buildings, could normally have been expected to contain an important town.

The primeval, empty site of Bath, as mythical Bladud or actual Iron Age man would have seen it, was scenically beautiful. But it was not a place to which prehistoric or mediaeval folk would normally have been drawn from the better drained hilltops and slopes to make a settlement of any note. With a watertable higher than nowadays the ground at river level would have been more marshy, and more prone to floods, than in later centuries. The river valley, at this point between Beechen Cliff and Lansdown, was awkwardly narrow; between the marshy ground and the steep slopes the inhabitable area was uninvitingly small. In each direction the valley so widened out as to be a more likely scene for habitation. For modest villages this tract of country would in time be reasonably good; Batheaston, Walcot, and Twerton duly proved it so. But it would not serve, one crucial factor excepted, for a populous town.

The making of legendary as of historic Bath was the gushing up, amid the bosky, uncleared scrub of the valley, of the hot mineral springs whose steamy effluence seeped up in a stretch of ground not much above the level of the Avon. It must always have been obvious that this belt of hot springs, like the more tepid well in the Clifton Gorge, sent up water of no ordinary quality. The Bladud legend suggests that its healing properties, at least for skin troubles, were used, and placed under divine tutelage, in prehistoric times. But no static settlement need have grown up by those hot springs in the period of Iron Age man. The local centre of habitation was not down in the valley, but up on the well fortified Solsbury Hill, whose name may still enshrine that of the Celtic deity held to be the guardian of the hot springs. In the last years before the Roman Conquest the thing for which the Romans best knew North Somerset was Mendip lead. It was this lead that was traded, before Claudius' invasion of A.D.43, between Britain and Roman Gaul. The swift occupation of the Mendip country suggests that quick control of the valuable lead

mines, not the hot springs in the deep, thinly peopled
Avon valley, chiefly drew the Roman army to the West.
Very soon, however, the region's other geological
distinguishing point attracted attention. With the
exploitation of the Waters of Sul there started the long
civilised career of Bath.

The thermal settlement of *Aquae Sulis* was a town much
unlike the others of Roman Britain. It was eventually
fortified, and in a district devoid of large towns it could
have gained some importance as a market centre. It
could have been a transit point for the important commodity of Mendip lead, a staging place and river
crossing on the Fosse Way, and a link in the communications of southern Britain, via the little port of *Abona**
and across the Severn estuary, to the legionaries and
civil population in Siluria. Yet it was really a town of
peculiar type. It was no legionary fortress or provincial
capital. First and foremost (as in its Georgian heyday)
fame came to *Aquae Sulis* as a spa, the chief settlement of
its type in Roman Britain. Some twenty-three acres in
extent, *Aquae Sulis* was small and unpopulous; Roman
Cambridge, a mere posting station on the Colchester to
Chester road, was larger in area. Yet the core of Roman
Bath, a rectangular area containing the baths and a
religious precinct with its small Corinthian temples,
was of more architectural note than most towns in this
most remote of the Empire's provinces.

The Baths themselves, a long series of plunges and
smaller rooms on each side of a great central bath, were
not built in one operation. The successive phases in
their building, in some ways still somewhat obscure but
certainly done at varying periods, can be studied, along
with many relics from here and elsewhere in Roman
Bath, if one visits the Baths themselves in their much
improved and redecorated state.

* Now Sea Mills within the area of modern Bristol.

3

In the first century A.D., not long after their conquest of southern Britain and certainly by the year 76,* the Romans started to build their *thermae* at Bath. The water, as they gladly found, was naturally hot, but they also included a deep, semi-circular, stone-seated bath for a specially recommended cold water treatment which had benefited the Emperor Augustus. What they mainly did was to provide buildings for the sequence of bathing as the Roman world knew and enjoyed it.

The central compartment of the baths at *Aquae Sulis* was a great rectangular plunge. A tepid, comforting swim in this open-air pool may at first have been all that was available. Soon, however, more plunges, and heated rooms for the sweating treatment now favoured in Romano-British society, were added at each end. It is in these additions that one can best follow the baths' build ing history of over two hundred years.

The great central bath, of all that has been excavated since the first discovery of 1755, is the part of the complex which is of the greatest architectural interest and most eloquent of past social glories (plate 1). Slender circular pillars upheld the cornice of a covered colonnade built round the central plunge; as in the Roman baths at Leicester little alcoves of alternately rectangular or curved plan opened out from this promenading space, their walls of excellent masonry being part of the main building's outer wall. Yet an open-air pool did not lastingly satisfy the Romanised Britons. Rectangular, well moulded plinths were added on each side of the column bases, and sturdier piers now upheld a shallow concave roof whose stone or concrete work had its weight relieved by the building in of box tiles. The aisles, like those of many Romanesque cathedrals in coming cen- turies, were strengthened by cross arches like concealed flying buttresses. At each end of the bathing hall the roof's

* The year of Bath's earliest dated inscription.

4

shallow curve allowed light and air to come in through a
lunette. Steps led, and still lead, into the grey-green
mineral water; below that opacity the pool's lining was
of still surviving sheets of Mendip lead.

At one end of the central bath one sees a charming
circular pool, which may once have been roofed with a
shallow dome. Beyond it are the hypocaust piers of some
rooms which may have been added later. East of the
central bath is the area only recently well lit and made
more intelligible to visitors. The semicircular cold bath,
with its stone seat, is an eloquent relic. Close by, another
rectangular plunge has seen, in its illuminated water, the
swift growth of a modern "tradition" whereby visitors
do as one does at the lovely Trevi fountain in Rome,
dropping coins as an earnest of another visit. Again to
the East, the successive levels of rebuilding and adaptation
can be seen. A sweating bath and then, on a later and
higher floor level still partly decorated with tesselated
pavements, several hypocaust rooms followed one upon
the other; the last, with their furnace arrangements,
were perhaps fitted out as late as the fourth century.

The baths of *Aquae Sulis* must have seemed impressive
when complete and in working order. Within Britain
they must have been of major consequence, giving *Aquae
Sulis* a special status. But only at a provincial level were
they really monumental. One could not compare them
to the great *thermae* of Rome, nor even, in the north-
western sector of the Empire, to the obviously imperial
scale and complexity of the two great baths whose ruins
are still notable in Trier, the *Augusta Treverorum* whence
Britain itself was ruled in the subdivided Empire of
Constantine.

For other Roman relics one turns to the collection now
well housed in the Baths Museum. Solinus, a topographer
of about 250 A.D., specially mentions the temple of
Minerva, not forgetting the curiosity of a perpetually

burning votive fire of Somerset coal. The chief deity of Roman Bath was really an amalgamation, the Celtic Sul being identified, in the politically convenient manner of the Roman Empire, with Minerva. Sul-Minerva's temple was an apt blend of Celtic and Classic elements. Its fluted columns, with excellent Corinthian capitals, were fully in the classic manner – along with fragments of fluted pilasters and carved cornices they proved how Britain, under Roman rule, got its first taste of sophistication in building. But the main pediment, above its four Corinthian columns, was of a provincial, ungrammatical steepness. In that pediment the famous Gorgon head of Minerva's shield, supported by winged Victories and accompanied by the goddess' helmet and a podgy little owl, has the flowing hair and fierce moustaches of Celtic inspiration. Other sculpture found in Bath is provincial in tone, or even anticipates Romanesque. But in one splendid relic, found in 1727 when Bath was just starting its expansion as a planned, sophisticated, neo-Roman city, we see finesse and beauty of a high order. The gilt-bronze head of Minerva was probably made in southern Gaul or North Italy, being brought to adorn the spa of Roman Britain. Above Minerva's serenely noble features the crown of the head is missing, and a helmet probably capped the whole. The classic dignity and quiet simplicity of this head make it, perhaps, the greatest single treasure of Bath, setting that tone of poise and taste which duly distinguished the Georgian city (frontispiece).

Other relics recalling Roman Bath are the altars of dedication and sepulchral slabs; their inscriptions, clearly cut and precisely placed in the historic fabric of the Roman Empire, tell us not only the names of those who set them up, but some of the widely scattered provinces whence these people came. A stone carver hailed from *Corinium* (Cirencester) in the Cotswolds. But some soldiers and civilians who came to *Aquae Sulis* and died

1. ROMAN BATHS; the Plunge Bath.

2. THE KING'S BATH; on the left, the Pump Room.

3. The Abbey from the South-West.

there were far more distant from their old homes. Some were from Belgium or eastern France, one man came from near Trier in the borderland between Gaul and Germany. A retired legionary probably hailed from Asia Minor, and a cavalryman, born at *Caurium* (Coria) in western Spain, served in a squadron recruited among the Vettones, hardy horsemen of that wild upland district of Roman Lusitania.

Of the houses, and other civilian buildings, we can tell less than we can of Roman Bath's cemeteries and bathing places, for their main traces lie buried below the modern town. But they certainly existed. So too, one may suppose, did a bridge to take the Fosse Way over the Avon. This crossing point, and some dwelling houses, were the things in *Aquae Sulis* which most probably outlasted the splendours of the baths, handing on an element of continuity into part at least of the long interlude between Roman provincial life and documented Saxon habitation.

Chapter II

DARK INTERLUDE

THE Romans, like William the Conqueror, completed their conquest of southern Britain within ten years. But the Saxon occupation of the same territory was more like a slow process of seepage than a swiftly executed military campaign. Not for some eighty years after the legions left Britain did the first Saxons land in what later became Wessex. That landing, in or near Southampton Water, was about 495 A.D. Not till about 560, in Ceawlin, do we find a single King of the West Saxons; this Ceawlin, along with another chieftain named Cuthwine, first brought Bath within Anglo-Saxon power. That was in 577; over a century and a half had passed since the end of Roman control.

Town life in Roman Britain had eventually tended to decline; *Aquae Sulis* may well have been touched by such a trend. Yet neither then, nor for some years after Britain ceased, politically speaking, to have effective links with the Graeco-Roman World, need we think of the spa as wholly disused. As at the Bristol Hotwells about 1830, the story was probably one of slow running down, not of sudden or final catastrophe. The Britons, still unsubdued and clinging to the relics of their Roman culture and to their Christian faith, long lived unchallenged in the West. They went back, so it seems, to something like the tribal subdivisions which prevailed before the Romans and which had continued, beneath the overriding framework of the "provinces" of late Roman Britain, round such

8

"county towns" as Caerwent or Cirencester. Each Roman town of any note may thus have become the more or less independent capital of the district around it. In this "cantonised" state of affairs three places in the West where a measure of town life lingered on were *Glevum* (Gloucester), *Corinium* (Cirencester), and Bath. The first and the third lay on rivers of some size and depth, the settlement of Cirencester on a little Cotswold stream not hard to ford. In Bath, we may guess, the scene was a sad shadow of the past. No soldiers from Spain or Asia, no provincial officials, no civilians and ladies from West Germany or Gaul frequented the slowly decaying baths. The Romano-Britons had the half-used *thermae* to themselves. When the Saxons closely threatened Bath the actual spa district of the little town may perhaps have been deserted, and Celtic Christians would have found scant use for the pagan temples and shrines. But a town, however small and seedy, could serve for simple trade, for communications, and as a centre for the wan relics of organised rule. So Bath is said, by the chronicler who later wrote of the slow process of Saxon conquest, to have been, like Cirencester and Gloucester, the seat of a British "King".

In the middle decades of the sixth century the Saxons of Wessex were steadily pressing the Britons still holding out in what are now Somerset and Gloucestershire. Well South of Bath, the wild tract of Selwood Forest had remained a barrier; behind it, in Camelot (perhaps Cadbury Camp near Yeovil) and Avalon "Arthurian" Britons for a time kept their Christianity and their faintly Romanised Celtic way of life. In Bath and in the Cotswold country the British position was less happy.*

Pushing up towards the Cotswolds and the rich Severn valley, Ceawlin and Cuthwine threatened both to

---

* For the Saxons in central Somerset and more to the West, *see* W. G. Hoskins "*The Westward Expansion of Wessex*", *1960*.

occupy new territory and to split the Britons in the West from their colleagues in the Midlands. The petty "Kings" of Bath, Cirencester, and Gloucester made bold to oppose them. These rulers, so we hear, had the names of Commagil, Condidan, and Farinmagil; they could, one feels, have fitted easily into a list of minor personages in "King Lear". Up in the south Cotswolds, near Dyrham in 577, a great battle raged. The Britons were shattered. The three kinglets were slain. Bath, Gloucester, and Cirencester all fell, and the conquerors swept unopposed into what later became Gloucestershire and Worcestershire. Wessex colonists called the Hwicce newly settled the land. To Bath, all recollections of *Aquae Sulis* being forgotten, there was given the name of Akemanceaster— "Sick Men's Town". For another century its story stays obscure. Now, perhaps, was its century of fullest desolation. A river crossing point, with a few poor houses in the rising, less muddy ground to the North of it, may have kept up a starveling continuity between the opulent past and the monastic future. These decades may also have seen the final decay of the Roman baths. A graphic account comes down in a poem composed some two centuries later. The bard, imaginatively mentioning "high-fretted pinnacles" which could hardly have graced any classical building, is clearly conditioned in his verses by the buildings of his own time. For he speaks of many "mead-halls" once supposed to have been full of melody ; more truthfully he refers to the wall which once encompassed the baths. Now, moreover, would surely have been the time to say that "the red hall sheddeth its tiles". The springs, however, remained, gushing hot and still healthful through the soggy ground which now harboured waterfowl and muddily shrouded the splendours of Roman Bath.

In this time of Bath's twilight desolation there came a change in the heptarchic balance of power. The Midland

Kingdom of Mercia became the most powerful Saxon realm in the South. The Cotswold country, right down to the Bristol Avon which is its true southern limit, became Mercian territory. The town of Bath (all *North* of the river) became part of Mercia to which it orographically belonged; within Mercia it may well have been the southern tip of the old "Winchcombeshire", taking in the Cotswold part of the present county, while the Severn Vale was grouped round Gloucester. The present county of Gloucestershire was created later, when Bath had gone into Wessex and so into Somerset, but had all our present counties and shires been defined so early as the eighth or nnth century Bath would not have been in Somerset but in Gloucestershire. For over twc centuries it was a Mercian town, and for church purposes under the Bishop of Worcester.*

It was a Mercian ruler, a Christian and anxious to erect missionary strongholds at strategic points in the part of Mercia under his care, who first established religious houses near river crossings whose dwellings lay amid the fragments of Roman towns. Osric, sub-king or viceroy of Mercia's Hwiccian province, is best known for his foundation at Gloucester; it was there, soon before the great abbey's Tudor dissolution, that the monks set up the tomb still seen on one side of the cathedral sanctuary. But this Osric was also, so it seems, responsible for the first religious house at Bath. An abbess first ruled it, and the date is given as 676. It would soon have come under the first of Worcester's bishops. Its career was chequered. By the time that Bath went into Wessex its régime had changed at least twice. Secular canons were there in 956 and they, it seems, were the men who built the church "with marvellous workmanship". In the 960's this religious house in the marches

---

* For more on Winchcombeshire, and on Bath's eventual transfer from Mercia to Wessex, *see* Chapter 2 of *Gloucestershire Studies*, ed. H. P. R. Finberg, 1957.

11

between the Wessex and Mercian provinces of a united
England had been caught up in the Benedictine revival
whose chief sponsor was that great Somerset man St.
Dunstan. It was in this Saxon abbey church, in 973, that
the ceremony of King Edgar's belated coronation was
staged.

I am not sure why fourteen years passed between
Edgar's accession and his crowning. What concerns me,
as a twentieth-century delineator of Bath, is the reason
for what seems, to our minds, an odd geographical choice.
Why Bath, and not Winchester or the more normal
Wessex crowning place of Kingston-on-Thames?
Political considerations, with Bath a border town
between Wessex and the Midland areas most free from
Danish influence, may have played their part. There
may also have been factors less rooted in politics than in
architecture.

A Charter of 957 is positive that the church at Bath
was of *mira fabrica* ; it seems clear that it was considered
out of the ordinary. In such a locality it would have been
of stone. In another sixteen years, when St. Dunstan
(by now Archbishop of Canterbury) was looking for a
church suitable for the holding of an indoor, fully
ecclesiastical ceremony of Coronation this newly built
church, now Benedictine and with its ordered worship
to this Benedictine Archbishop's liking, could have
suited his purpose far better than any other church in
politically desirable northern Wessex. It could easily
have been more spacious than the then unimposing
abbey church at Glastonbury. The church at Wells,
though now the Somerset's bishop's cathedral, was
almost certainly a poor, rudimentary structure. Bath
Abbey, I feel, was in 973 well ahead of its neighbours. It
was probably basilican, aisled with round-arched
arcades and with short transepts and a sanctuary. It could
have resembled, and anticipated, the basilican cathedral

soon built at Sherborne.* For the large congregation which a Coronation gathering of magnates implied, it could have been decisively suitable. Such, we may imagine, was the Saxon Romanesque abbey church of "Hatum Bathum", modest by later standards and perhaps about the size of Bath's modern, basilican Catholic church dedicated to St. Alphege, that great Bathonian of late Saxon times. It could, however, have dominated the little riverside town, with its still steaming springs, which changed little till well after the Norman conquest.

The Normans brought only a partial transfer in the lordship of Bath. Such parts of the Borough as had been in monastic hands remained, like church estates elsewhere, in clerical hands. The abbey mill still ground the monks' corn; the riverside meadows pastured their cattle. Most of the little Borough, along with its Saxon mint, was a royal possession by the time of Domesday; one Hugh "The Interpreter" is mentioned as holding property, in Bath itself and out at Bathampton. The little town, with hardly more than a thousand people, had seen few physical changes since the Normans had come. It was of no great strategic note, and the area was thinly peopled, so no royal castle towered above its walls and houses. It was from the Church, not the King, that mediaeval Bath got the greatest of its buildings.

* For this, *see* the West Dorset volume of the Royal Commission on Historic Monuments.

13

Chapter III

MONASTIC CITY

THE reign of William Rufus started tragically for Bath. In a few months rebellion broke out among many of the new king's magnates. Bath was burnt and plundered by those of the conspirators who made of the new castle at Bristol a base whence they harried much of the West. About the same time Aelfsige, the Abbot of Bath, passed away and left the field clear for drastic changes. Town and monastery alike soon took on a new character which endured till the Reformation.

The Somerset bishopric also fell vacant soon after the death of Abbot Aelfsige. The new bishop was John of Tours, a French priest who was in favour with Rufus and was also well known as a physician. His, very largely, was the decision whereby the monastic church at Bath became, for some decades, the sole cathedral of Somerset. The king gave the new bishop his royal grant both of the abbey estates and of the lordship of the ravaged town. This move, so it seems, was all part of the Norman church policy whereby bishops' sees located in small or remote places were moved to towns whose actual or potential importance was greater, or where town walls gave better protection against ravage and invasion. Not that Somerset had much to offer which could easily be preferred to the tiny city of Wells. Bridgwater was not yet enough in the Somerset picture. Ilchester was small, awkward, and remote amid its floodprone marshlands. Taunton had long been a large, rich, and

important estate of the Bishop of Winchester ; such a
prelate would hardly have welcomed another bishop in
his town. Bath, as we can assume from Domesday, had
hardly more people than a large village nowadays. It
was not the centre of a notable or populous area, and the
new bishop may not have foreseen how soon, in this
district of the lower Avon valley, it would be over-
shadowed by the growing port and trading town of
Bristol. It must, however, have seemed reasonably
preferable to Wells, and for a bishop with medical
interests its hot and healing springs may have been an
added attraction. So Bath became John of Tours' choice.
The transfer once made, in 1090-91, there remained the
problem, soon also tackled in the neighbouring diocese of
Worcester, of a more spacious and worthy cathedral.

The new bishop may have found the Saxon cathedral
much damaged by the recent rebellion. In any case,
he pulled it down and wholly replaced it by a great
Norman Romanesque church. John of Tours had his
new cathedral built in the usual manner of the Norman
period. A long nave of eight bays was probably ended
by a western facade whose vast single arch would have
been like that still seen at Tewkesbury. Inside, however,
the sturdy arcades seem not to have had the very tall
cylindrical pillars which gave distinction to the Abbeys
of Tewkesbury, Gloucester, and Pershore. The piers and
arches would have been of the more modest height seen
at Ely or Norwich; above them the triforium stage
probably had pairs of small openings, each pair within
a single retaining arch. East of the central tower, a
similar arrangement would have been seen in the presbytery ; the precise plan of the eastern limb has been lost,
but it would have somehow ended in a rounded apse.
Decoration, at least in the earlier and eastern part of the
church, must have been simple and restrained. But
somewhere within the monastery precincts carved work

existed of very high quality. Two twelfth-century capitals which still survive, imitation Corinthian with figure carving worked into the designs, are among the best things seen in Bath. South of the church were the cloisters, the chapter house and dormitories, and the usual, close-knit group of other monastic buildings. A bishop's house was also there, to the West of the main complex of the cathedral priory.

The long, low Norman church must dominate our picture of mediaeval Bath. Its massive piers and thick walls must have made it seem sturdy and durable. But Norman masonry was apt to be weaker than it looked, and the story was often of poor repair and decay. Nor was the convent rich enough to carry out really drastic repairs and rebuildings on its church.

The topographer William "of Worcester", who wrote in the fifteenth century and left priceless details on the towns (especially his own home town of Bristol) and churches of his time, says that Bath Cathedral was about 290 feet long. He was, perhaps, a little on the short side, but one point seems likely from his account. The Lady Chapel, when built, was not at the Norman church's eastern end. The work was done about 1260. One pictures an attractive building, with shafts and a vault, and perhaps with early tracery in the windows. Ordinations were sometimes held in it, and in 1499 a new prior was there presented to his office. The mediaeval Lady Chapels of England's greater churches were not, however, invariably at the East end. Where the slope of the ground, or the borders of the site, dictated they could run East from a transept. The beautiful new chapel of the Abbey (now the Cathedral) at Bristol could have given the Bath monks a good precedent for such a plan ; a similar site was later chosen at Peterborough and Ely.

Apart from the Lady Chapel no basic change seems ever to have been mdae in the ground plan of Bath

Cathedral ; the bishops, as a rule, preferred their more central Palace and Cathedral at Wells. As at Gloucester and Durham Norman windows could have been filled with tracery and some were probably replaced by larger ones. Bishop Bubwith (1407–24) built a chantry chapel in the nave; we may guess that it resembled his lovely "stone cage" in the nave at Wells. Later still, Bishop Bekynton, a great builder at Wells, gave the monks a new, presumably more comfortable dormitory.

Other religious foundations arose in the little city. St. John the Baptist's Hospital was founded, in 1174, by Bishop Reginald. His aim was to help the sick and poor to benefit from the healing waters ; those waters, in the Cross Bath whose pool had a cross rising clear above it, were just by his buildings. Another early hospital was that of St. Mary Magdalene for lepers, high perched on the hill whose main feature is Beechen Cliff. The chapel, rebuilt about 1490 and restored after bomb damage in 1942, is urban Bath's best relic of the days before the early Tudor "Abbey". No Friary was ever founded to keep these hospitals company. The parish churches of St. Mary de Stalls, St. James, St. Michael outside Northgate, St. Mary's close inside the same gate, and St. Michael's inside Westgate, were there to meet the needs of the laity. None of them is likely to have been of much size, but Georgian prints show that St. James' had a pleasant fifteenth-century tower, with one pinnacle rising well above the other three in a manner common in North Somerset and the area of Bristol.

The city itself, a Borough with royal charters starting in 1189 and a Mayor at least from 1230, was of some standing and prestige. But its size and population seem hardly to have kept pace with its civic status, and mediaeval Bath, frequented for its waters by those with rheumatics and skin diseases but not so heavily as to grow into a really large town, seems to have suffered from those disadvantages of site we have earlier noticed. It was soon surpassed by its neighbour Bristol, a town so placed as to be the chief port and *entrepot* both for the West and Midlands. Bath's population, in the Poll Tax year of 1377, seems not to have reached a thousand. It may thus have been smaller than at the time of Domesday, and recovery may well have been painfully slow from the Black Death of 1349 and the plague's sharp repetition in 1361. One redeeming factor, however, was the Westcountry cloth trade, by now of gathering note in Somerset and the neighbouring counties. Among the cloth-workers of this time we have the buxom, immortal figure of Chaucer's Wife of Bath, finding time between her numerous pilgrimages to surpass the skilled Flemish weavers of Ypres and Ghent. She may, in fact, have hailed from Twerton, down river from the main city and long a noted centre of her craft. I like to imagine that the church door at which she took her five successive husbands was the fine Norman portal of Twerton's parish church, preserved in its early Victorian rebuilding and the best Norman thing still seen in the present city.

For the Norman Cathedral, above ground, has almost wholly gone. By the last years of the fifteenth century its dilapidation had become desperate. Nothing would do but its total replacement. The building then started is of great importance both in itself, and as showing architectural trends running in England's late mediaeval monasticism. It also throws a sidelight on early Tudor politics.

In 1495 a new bishop came to Bath and Wells in the person of Oliver King. He had already, for three years, been bishop of Exeter, but his court appointments had not allowed him to reside. Under Edward IV this courtier cleric had been chief secretary to the King. Richard III had him put in the Tower, but Henry VII restored him and he stood high in the favour of the first

Tudor monarch. In 1497 his Somerset diocese was twice disturbed by rebellion, for the Cornish rebels traversed the county on their march to Blackheath, and Perkin Warbeck got as far as Taunton before his political collapse. In the former uprising several leading county figures, both lay and clerical, were severely compromised and got heavily fined. Bishop Oliver King, in another two years resigning his secretaryship at Court, came down to Somerset, and this most loyal friend and servant of the new dynasty then resided in his diocese to keep a watchful eye on a county where disaffection and heresy alike gave some cause for concern.

In 1499 the bishop gave much of his attention to the Cathedral Priory at Bath. In April a monk named William Bird was made sacrist, with responsibility for the church's fabric. In the summer the bishop set in motion a long, formal visitation of the convent. Late in August, Prior Cantlow having died, William Bird succeeded him. Bishop and prior now closely colla-borated over the replacement of the tottering cathedral. The bishop, so one gathers from the Elizabethan Sir John Harington, was spurred on by a dream in which he saw angels climbing up and down ladders to the Trinity at the top. At the bottom an olive tree had its trunk girt with a crown; the picture would strongly have recalled the tree at Bosworth with the dead Richard III's crown lying beneath it. A voice cried out "Let an Olive estab-lish the Crown, and let a King restore the Church." Dream or no dream, the elements of the story made the motivation of the new church's unusual western facade.

First, however, an important planning decision was made; it was not without precedent in the hard-headed, commonsense monastic architecture of an age when monks were fewer, and when most monastic naves no longer had parochial functions. For when in 1309 the abbey church of Milton in Dorset was burnt down the new choir and transepts were laid out on part only of the long Norman nave. A new nave was intended, but excavation has shown that it was never built. At St. Augustine's, Bristol the eastern limb was replaced about this same time, but though a new nave was started it may never have been completed. At Bath, King and Bird decided, while temporarily keeping in use the old Norman tower space and eastern limb, to build a complete new church, cruciform but much shorter than the old one and cut down to the needs of a medium-sized convent in a city full of parish churches. It was to occupy no more than the site of the Norman nave; only at the West would their new facade project a little beyond the old cathedral's limits. But that Norman cathedral still powerfully influences the plan of the early Tudor "Abbey". For the slender pillars of its nave and choir arcades rest on foundations which once supported the piers of the Norman nave, the simple early Tudor bays corresponding in length to those that went before them. So too, the piers of the tower rest on the foundations of *one* Norman bay; the Perpendicular tower is thus not square but rectangular, the chief present-day legacy from the ground plan of the great Norman cathedral. Other visible relics of that church are the bases of its western crossing piers and the rounded arch which led from its southern nave aisle to the adjoining transept. What was planned for the monastic buildings we cannot certainly say. But most of them, including the new dormitory, would readily have been kept. The new South transept would, however, have cut across the old northern cloister walk. So a new cloister range may have been so planned as to leave the church (as at Milton) a mainly free-standing building, with a vestibule to connect the monks' living quarters with the large early Tudor doorway by which one now enters the Jacobean vestry from the South choir aisle.

The architecture of the new cathedral was innovating and important. There was no question of regional design. Even the tower, had its corner turrets and intermediate pinnacles been finished more or less as they were last century, would have been closer in spirit to the contemporary Magdalen tower at Oxford than to those of the Westcountry abbeys or the tall western towers of Somerset's parish churches. The statesman-bishop patronised two designers of the Court school whose work for the king he already well knew. Bath Abbey is no more regional in its architecture than are the Palladian buildings of the Georgian town. (plate 3)

The designers employed by Bishop King were the brothers Robert and William Vertue; William, who outlived his brother, was specially expert at designing vaults. Their church at Bath has an eastern limb of three bays, a narrow crossing, and a five-bay nave. Its arcades are the simplest of early Tudor work. There is no attempt at a triforium, and the interior decoration of the walls and windows is most sparing and must have been conveniently economical. More exciting, with their sharply pointed arches resembling those of King's College chapel at Cambridge, are the great transomed windows of the clerestory. The West window too is of a generous size, and so anxious were the designers for the utmost inflow of light that the great East window, like one in the *Hooglandschekerk* at Leiden in the Netherlands, is set with its main arch contained in a square-headed frame.

For more spectacular effects we turn to the West front, the townward side of the church. There, along with the Twelve Apostles and a sculptured rendering of the bishop's dream of angels and ladders, we find devices which also make of this western facade, more modestly than at King's or in the royal chapels, a political demonstration in stone. For the arms and supporters of

Henry VII are just below the niche which again holds his statue. The crown-girt olive trees of the dream (which could also be the tree of Bosworth) are on the outermost buttresses, while high on the facade, and below the large statues of St. Peter and St. Paul which flank the western doorway with its two renderings of the Five Wounds,* the crowned rose and portcullis do honour to the new dynasty (plate 5).

More exciting still, and more typically the work of their designers, are the vaults of the choir and its aisles; those in the nave are good Victorian copies by Sir Gilbert Scott. Bath Abbey was notable, in its own time, as the first *wholly new* church on a major scale to be designed from the start to have fan vaults across its main compartments; the vaults at Sherborne Abbey, though a little older, rest partly on earlier masonry. The great vault of the choir does not, as in the somewhat later vault at King's chapel which is often compared to it, have its bays marked clearly from each other by great transverse arches. The great cones of its structure overlap the bays and thus give a more "unified", to my mind more agreeable effect. It was this vault that the Vertues regarded so proudly as to tell the bishop that there should "be noone so goodly neither in England nor in France". More interesting still, and extremely beautiful, are the smaller fan vaults in the aisles. For along the centre line are delicate pendants, foreshadowing with an astonishing likeness those which the Vertues later set along the centre lines of the main chapel and aisles of the Henry VII chapel at Westminster (plate 4). The decoration of these lovely vaults is almost wholly heraldic. Benefactors and other Benedictine monasteries in Wessex are there along with the keys of St. Peter and the sword of St. Paul in Bath Cathedral Priory's own arms. A completion date

* A particularly popular device in these last decades before the Reformation ; they occur again in the vault of the North choir aisle.

4. FANS AND PENDANTS; in the Abbey, South Choir Aisle.

5. THE ABBEY; the West Door.

6. ABBEY CHURCH HOUSE;
Elizabethan Fireplace.

is suggested by the arms of Cardinal Adriano di Castello, a not very reputable functionary at the Papal Court who was the absentee bishop of Bath and Wells from 1504 to 1518. The eastern limb, at all events, must have been finished before his deposition, and one assumes that new stalls were provided, or the old ones moved temporarily from the choir of the Norman cathedral. In 1525 Prior Bird died. His early Tudor chantry, with its own little fan vault and the cove above its altar adorned by a grouping of Bird's arms and the *pontificalia insignia* which the Prior of Bath was entitled to use, is delightfully placed between the sanctuary and the South aisle. Canopied niches, little birds, and the initials W.B. form part of its decoration. One of this chantry's main spandrels has a mutilated Annunciation. In another, so it seems, a Centaur is abducting a classical heroine. The Renaissance, indeed, was at hand; not long after Bird's death the dissolution deprived Bath of its monastery and the unfinished church of its cathedral status.

Additional note, February 1980

In the autumn of 1979 the Bath Archaeological Trust sponsored excavations in Orange Grove, East of the Abbey and on the site of the Norman cathedral's transepts and presbytery. They proved that beyond a short aisled presbytery, the church's sanctuary had a "periapsidal" end, with an arcade behind the High Altar, and with an ambulatory and three projecting chapels as at Gloucester and Norwich. No convincing evidence was found for the position or style of the Lady Chapel, but the excavation substantially bore out the length given by William "of Worcester" for the cathedral without that chapel. It seems that the nave of the Norman cathedral, and the present church, occupied the site of the Anglo-Saxon abbey church.

Chapter IV

VICISSITUDES

THE age of the later Tudors, and of the Stuarts, was a time of much transition, and of some tragedy, in Bath. We first see the passing of old and splendid landmarks, with economic straitness only partly made good by an enlargement of status. But by the last years of the seventeenth century better trends were unmistakable and lasting, and Bath stood on the eve of its greatest, most fashionable glory.

The cathedral monastery, like the one at Coventry, was dissolved in 1539. It was about this time that Leland paid his antiquarian visit to Bath, taking notes of baths and Roman relics, noting also that the eastern limb of the great Norman church still stood in ruins beyond the substantially finished segment of its late Perpendicular successor, roofless and desolate and with weeds luxuriant round its builder's tomb in the deserted presbytery. The eastern limb of the new church, vaulted but seemingly without its complement of pinnacles, was soon in little better case. For the city authorities turned down the offer of the building for use as a parish church. The valuable lead was therefore stripped from the roof. The glass (again with valuable lead) was taken from the windows and the monastery bells were melted down. So the new choir was no longer weatherproof, and the nave had never even been roofed. The great church, despoiled and reduced to a shell, stood high amid the houses as a gaunt reproach. The monastery buildings, church and

24

all, were sold by the Crown to one Humphrey Colles, who at once resold them to Matthew Colthurst. The monastic buildings were destroyed, while the land in their close neighbourhood came eventually to the Pierrepont family who were of some note in the development of Georgian Bath. The church, so it seemed, might in time have suffered the obliteration which befell the monastic church at Coventry. Yet Bath, in a long spell of fits, starts, and hesitations, was in the end more fortunate than the Midland city in the rescue of its erstwhile co-cathedral.

The story takes us through most of the reign of Elizabeth I, and that of James I; what happened, in some respects, was like the restoration process at Abbey Dore in Herefordshire which ended so happily in "Laudian" times. In 1560 Edmund Colthurst, the son of Matthew Colthurst, gave the Corporation what was later called the "carcass" of the church. Something similar had been done, soon after the Dissolution, at Malmesbury. For a rich clothier named Stumpe, while using some monastic building to gather working weavers under one roof (thus anticipating the factory system) had given to the townspeople Malmesbury Abbey's nave which they then used as their parish church. But the Bathonians long looked their gift horse in the mouth, and St. Mary de Stalls, repaired and refurnished as occasion offered, continued as the civic church. Then in 1572 Peter Chapman, a soldier born of a leading clothier family in Bath, repaired the North aisle of the choir. Most of the church still lay desolate; loads of stone would at times be taken from its gauntly roofless nave. Had the monastery church, like those at Keynsham or Winchcombe, entirely disappeared it could well have passed out of mind. But it still towered high over the mean little city as a mute reproach. So it seemed, in 1574, to Elizabeth I when she visited Bath on a western progress

25

which also included Longleat and Bristol. She strongly suggested that the Abbey should be put in good order. In another two years Letters Patent gave permission to the Corporation, only lately busy on finishing its pillared Market House, to raise money from outside Bath. They also spent a little themselves, on such items as timber, tiling, and iron. New roofs arose over the existing fan vaults and a new fan vault, adorned with the City arms and still seen in the Abbey, was put over the crossing. Another fan vault, and some structural work, completed the South transept; hence the date 1576 still seen on a buttress. The Corporation became patrons of the "Stalls", now the "Abbey" living. Now at last it was clearly intended that the one-time monastic church should become Bath's main parochial place of worship. The transepts and the choir were fitted up for staid Anglican worship. Important donors aided local endeavours. A key figure was Elizabeth's chief minister Lord Burghley. He was at Bath to take the waters in 1592, and his personal steward Thomas Bellot was a Bathonian, the founder of an almshouse in the city, and a generous helper of the Abbey. He aroused his master's interest, so that the great Lord Treasurer was among those who aided the slowly progressing work.

The credit for the slow saving of Bath Abbey goes to clothier families as well as to local gentry and the growing throng of eminent visitors. For the cloth trade, as Leland had seen, was in Bath and all the West a growing element in the local economy. Its ups and downs were soon seen in the prosperity or depression of the whole Avon basin. Its wellbeing, like that of the port of Bristol, largely turned on shipments to Spain and Portugal. So when in the 1580's the Spanish war became a firm reality it brought to this part of the West very little of the glory and glamour which came to Plymouth and its Devon heroes. Elizabeth's favourite Lord Leicester was at Bath,

7.   GREEN STREET and ST. MICHAEL'S STEEPLE.

8. THE OLD GRAMMAR SCHOOL, circa 1749.

9. A PARADE;
North Parade Buildings, c.1742.

for the waters, in 1587.* He wrote to Burghley of "great decay of the towns and distress of the people for want of work". Prosperity, as it happened, could only be assured to Bath by the growing influx of bathers and drinkers.

Yet something, the Abbey apart, seems none the less to have been done to improve the mien of the "poor and proud" little city once the Queen had honoured it in person. We hear, in a letter some years later than 1574, of fine houses for *victualling and lodging*. Increasing crowds of visitors, and their rumbustious retinues of servants, may have prompted the Queen's Government to grant Bath its important Charter of 1590, formally incorporating the city and for its better local administration creating it a "sole city of itself", in other words a "county borough" quite separate from the Somerset Justices in their distant meeting places at such towns as Taunton or Ilchester. The city's boundaries were also enlarged; it now included the whole area down to the river's loop and stretched uphill into the still rural parish of Walcot.

The reign of James I saw many notable Bath events. Work on the Abbey went forward about the time of the new King's accession. Thomas Bellot had a timber roof put above the South transept's vault, and other benefactors came forward. As only the eastern limb was available for worship the western doorway gaped empty and unused. So new entrances were made in the choir aisles. One of these, a doorway clearly later than the early Tudor monastic work, was given by Jeffrey Flower of Norton St. Philip; his arms and initials are there on tiny little spandrel shields. More important, from 1608 onwards, were the operations set in train by a new Bishop of Bath and Wells.

James Montagu, who now came to Somerset, had had

* He was on his way for another visit when he died in the Armada year of 1588 ; his journeying letter to the Queen was the last she ever had from him.

a career of some note at Cambridge and as Dean of Lichfield and Worcester. As a young, and strikingly handsome don he had been a fellow of Christ's, but in 1596 his uncle Sir John Harington of Exton had him made first Master of Sidney. In this capacity (his College grounds being due to benefit) he was largely responsible for the famous Cambridge watercourse of "Hobson's" Conduit. When James I journeyed South to his English throne Montagu was on a deputation from Cambridge to greet the new sovereign on his way. The Master of Sidney caught the King's eye, and as masculine good looks were a passport to the favour of James I the path of promotion lay easy before him. Once in his Somerset diocese he was much pained by the still uncompleted condition of Bath Abbey. His distant relative, Sir John Harington of Kelston, strongly urged him to its final roofing and fitting out for service. Donations now flowed in from far and wide. The nave's empty shell was covered with three panelled plaster ceilings. A fine stone pulpit, richly carved, was installed in 1612. By 1616, when the bishop moved to Winchester, the work was done. A crowning gift, from his brother Sir Henry, was the superb pair of oaken western doors, richly carved with Renaissance mantling and scrollwork, and thrice adorned with the family heraldry; it is now the best relic of a great act of reparation. Nobler still, when Montagu died in 1618, was the tomb set up in Bath Abbey, with which church his name was best linked. Of alabaster and marble, girt round with an iron railing and splendidly heraldic, it has at each end a short entablature on two graceful Corinthian columns. Between those terminals there lies, high poised, the bishop's effigy, arrayed in the Mantle of the Garter and well displaying the handsome features which had charmed England's first Stuart King. The sculptors of this masterpiece were immigrants from the Low Countries settled close to the Bishop of

Winchester's Southwark mansion, William Cuer, and Nicholas Johnson whose younger brother made Shakespeare's memorial at Stratford.

Good omens for Bath's social future came with some royal patronage. James I himself was never in the city, but Bath had three visits, expressly for taking its waters, from Anne of Denmark, his pleasure-loving Queen. In her honour the Queen's Bath, built close to the original cistern, got its name, while just to the West a mullioned lodging house, in 1618, paid honour to the Queen-Consort. For in the curious manner of those days (as one still sees at Castle Ashby, Northamptonshire and Oriel College, Oxford) the Roman capitals of a complimentary inscription were treated as a balustrade silhouetted against the sky. Royal favour soon brought more visitors, and by the 1620's the bathing of both sexes together in the older baths caused scandal and unavailing schemes for their segregation. In 1624 the King's Bath was fancifully edged by the strapwork balustrade which is partly there to-day (plate 2). Yet Bath shows little now of the buildings seen in the seventeenth century. The chief secular relic of the Elizabethan town is the much restored Abbey Church House, gabled and mullioned and early inhabited by one of the famous local family of the Hungerfords; its towering chimney-piece well typifies that age of opulent, rather barbaric Renaissance display (plate 6). The gabled houses of Lilliput Alley, with the shallowest of fireplace arches, seem more likely to be post-Dissolution than late mediaeval. Broad Street, once a clothmakers' quarter, is a town extension of the Stuart era, a fireplace and a few mullioned windows surviving to prove its date. At the foot of Holloway a gabled house has windows still showing the stumps of cut away mullions, while one or two houses with mullioned fenestration lie just off the Twerton road.

The Civil War found Bath a city of mainly royalist

leanings. In the summer of 1643 it was nearly the scene of a pitched battle. For the King's Cornish army, on a hot July day, stormed up the slopes of Lansdown's northern end, losing their revered leader Sir Bevil Grenville and many of the rank and file as they strove to dislodge the entrenched Parliament forces under Sir William Waller. The Puritans, in the end, were those who drew down into Bath, but tactically the battle was a draw, soon followed, at Roundway near Devizes, by the Royalist victory which for two years gave Charles I the control of nearly all the West. For Waller his Bath sojourn was an ironic experience, for there in the Abbey was what he had planned as his tomb, set up before 1634 with its canopy and fine alabaster figures of Waller and his first wife. But he married again, and found eventual burial in London.

In Charles II's time the cloth trade continued to be of note in Bath. Yet more and more the little city grew famous as a locally and nationally important spa. Fecundity was thought to be encouraged by a dip in the waters which also assuaged gout and skin trouble. So in 1663, when anxious for the birth of a legitimate child, Charles II brought Queen Catherine to Bath; his hopes, as one knows, were in vain. The party was there for some days, with visits as well to Longleat, Badminton, and Bath's larger neighbour Bristol. More visitors followed in the royal wake. National figures apart, Bath was the obviously favoured summer rendezvous of the western gentry. So when in 1680 Monmouth's political tour of Wessex brought him first of all to Bath he could readily expect to find at the waters many of those with whom a rendezvous was needed for planning and discussion. But in Bath itself the Exclusionists and Monmouthites found few supporters. In the Monmouth campaign of 1685 not only was the city held firmly for the King, but its outskirts were the assembly ground for the various units of the regular army which could now move, a tactically united force, to shadow and shepherd the dwindling rebels to their doom.*

Yet physically speaking Bath still fell far behind its status as England's chief watering place. John Evelyn, in 1654, had found its streets "narrow, uneven, and unpleasant"; though later visitors, including Pepys, had better things to say of the paving and buildings, there are no rhapsodies about social activities. There were, indeed, a few tree-lined walks and some facilities for bowls, but none of the organised "Spa life" that came with a rush in the next century. So much so that in 1683 the sleepy little cathedral city of Wells was reckoned by the Somerset Justices to be a better place for the Assizes than Bath which "had not so good accommodation for entertainments".

Yet Bath was well frequented, and often by the highest in the land. Bishops often came there, and the Lord Chancellor, so the papers of the Harley family tell us, was there in 1682. Queen Catherine, now Queen Dowager, was there again in 1686. Lodgings were hard to find, and boredom bred many quarrels and intrigues. Another royal visit was in 1687, when James II came with Queen Mary of Modena who bathed in the "select" waters of the Cross Bath and held it in their favour when she duly "found herself breeding" with the Old Pretender. The future Queen Anne was there about the same time and again, with civic bellringing to greet her, in 1692. Her favour would duly be decisive for Bath's lasting social glory. But as the century ended, with Dutch William still on the throne, there were few signs of physical or social expansion. Our picture, well shown in the map of 1694 made by Joseph Gilmore, a mathematics teacher of Bristol, is still of a little city nearly all confined within the close circuit of the mediaeval walls which nine years before had defied Monmouth's herald.

* For more on Bath in the Monmouth Rebellion, *see* Bryan Little, *The Monmouth Episode*, 1956, Chapter 7.

Chapter V

SPA TRIUMPHANT

QUEEN Anne, as reigning sovereign, stayed twice at
Bath, in 1702 and 1703. Some mitigation assuaged
what was, eventually, her incurable agony of gout and
dropsy. For a correspondent of Robert Harley said, of
her trial of the waters in 1703, that she was "pretty well
of the gout". These royal visits were not unlike those of
previous rulers and princes. State business was conducted
in the long hours left free from quaffing and wallowings
The inevitable throng of "Quality" was present. But
what mattered more for Bath's future, in these first year.
of a new century, was not so much the patronage of the
Queen, but the coming of the man who brought organised "fun and games" to Bath, and who would duly be
hailed as its social "King".

It was in 1705 that Richard Nash, a young Welshman
of little previous distinction, but of known talent in the
supervision of gambling and of other social activities,
first came to Bath, the greatest, perhaps, of many non-
Bathonians who have built up the modern city. His luck,
in other matters as well as gambling, was in. He was soon
the assistant of Captain Webster, the somewhat graceless
Master of Ceremonies. Webster soon died in a duel and
the Corporation, whose right it was to appoint a successor, gave Nash the post. For some forty years "Beau"
Nash set the social, though not the architectural, tone of
what was now, without serious challenge, Britain's
premier spa.

Beau Nash is so famous a figure in Bath's story that no detailed account of his activities is needed. He became a legend in his lifetime. Innumerable anecdotes were told of his doings and sayings. For a man of his background and social standing his was an amazing achievement. An obscure South Walian, of a respectable but non-armigerous family,* a failure at Oxford and as a budding lawyer, none the less won acceptance among the highest in the land. In an age when rank was fantastically important he made royal personages, dukes, and the whole range of the aristocracy submit to his will. He must have had a most powerful, winning personality, and a quite astonishing ability to "get away with it". John Wesley, so it seems, was one of the few who scored smartly off Nash in the heyday of his ascendancy. The Beau's great tragedy was that he long outlived the palmy days of his wealth and social acceptance. Born under Charles II he died, aged eighty-seven, in the reign of George III. By the time he was sixty he had done much, not only for the city of his adoption and for Tunbridge Wells, but for the whole fabric of England's social life.

Nash's activities in Bath were manifold. He saw to it that lodgings were improved, though one must realise that over twenty years of his rule had gone by before decisive action was started to give Bath large quantities of accommodation really suited to the dignity of such a spa. Mindful, one may suppose, of his predecessor's sad fate, he severely discountenanced the fighting of duels; such encounters, if they still happened, were apt to be well outside the city borders. The theatre first flourished at Bath under Nash's social regime and so, to the Beau's profit, did supervised gambling, a questionable activity but better that way than if it had been allowed

* Despite the word *armiger* in the Latin of his posthumous mural monument in the Abbey, Nash seems to have had no coat of arms. The cartouche on the monument is a symbolic picture, showing the hand of Death striking down a king's crown.

to run utterly to riot. Nash's coming to Bath could indeed have led to the city's becoming a very Alsatia of trickery, for in the year which followed the Beau's arrival Baron Robert Price, a legal friend of Robert Harley, reported that "about 50 known gamesters and sharpers" had come from London. But Nash, who had little to learn of the ways of such folk, seems to have had some real success in curbing their worst exploits. It appears, if the anecdotes are true, that the good-natured Beau did what he could, by various strategems, to save the more foolish of Bath's patrons from themselves, extending over those under his sway a general, avuncular protection which served many in good stead. More notable, by such means as his firm regulation of the ever more popular balls and assemblies, was the polished social pattern which spread, over those of all conditions and provenance, among the upper and middle class patrons of Nash's Bath.

What Bath really did for Georgian England was a great work, in architecture as in social manners, of standardisation. Provincial and local barriers were loosened. The people of the upper and middle classes were brought together, as never before, from all parts of the realm. The higher aristocracy, through Court life and the House of Lords, already knew each other. The House of Commons and the two Universities, for those who reached them, had helped in the same process of mixing. But not, by any means, for all the middling gentry, not for the rising professional or commercial classes, and not for their womenfolk. Yet at Bath, the national resort, the Squire Westerns of Wessex, with their ladies and marriagable children, could meet, and talk, and flirt, with the small gentry of East Anglia or the Midlands, or even with their rougher brethren of the far North. Intermarriage thus followed between families from widely separate provinces. Polite manners little known, so far, in the provincial Assize and Quarter

10. Pierrepont Place;
Doorway of the Linleys'
House.

11. In Gay Street;
Mrs. Piozzi's House.

12.   In Beaufort Square.

13.   WESTON CUT; Bridge of 1728.

Sessions towns could at Bath be diffused more readily than in London, a place seldom frequented by many smaller gentry. London accents kept pace with London manners, coming down to the Somerset meeting ground on the lips of Bath's more eminent visitors. England's local dialects, much used till now by provincial gentry gave way (with some loss of variety and colour) to a more standard tone among those who thought themselves "gentry" or "Quality".

At a higher social level Bath long stayed virtually supreme. Tunbridge Wells, or Scarborough, or such foreign resorts as Aachen or Spa, still attracted some visitors. But Bath still had no serious rivals in provincial England. The Bristol Hotwells, though important and much frequented by people of the same rank as Bath's more eminent patrons, were complementary to Bath and not its real rival, a summer spa which could, as one sees in "Humphrey Clinker" and the Bristol newspapers, pass visitors and tradesmen to Bath as winter set in. Cheltenham (not discovered as a spa till 1716) and Leamington had yet to reach their peak of importance. The seaside habit, though in time, at Weymouth, given early impetus by Ralph Allen and other Bathonians, had hardly started when Nash was "King" in Bath. So Bath was dominant, and performed its social function. Almost everyone who mattered in Georgian England was there sooner or later. One thing worth noting, but not enough to spoil the running, was that none of the four Georges ever went there as a reigning monarch.

There were, however, two sides of the Bath picture; very early in Nash's time we see how visits could doubly affect patrons. Of the spa's new popularity there could be little doubt. The neighbouring Duke of Beaufort kept an eye (high Tory political as well as social) on the place. Ducal visitors from elsewhere were also forthcoming, along with many lower graded aristocrats. The place became very expensive, with lodgings still at a premium. Early in 1707 a friend of the Harleys remarked that "it becomes a fashion to winter here"; others continued the older habit of a summer sojourn. Quarrels and intrigues flared up in plenty. If one great lady sponsored a play there were others who would not darken the doors of the theatre. Balls, by 1711, were a twice weekly function and apt to be noisy and stuffy; it was, however, "a crime" not to appear in public. Some patrons, Lord Chief Justice Parker for example or a canon of Christ Church, Dr. William Stratford, firmly believed in Bath's waters. Others, the eminent Dr. Radcliffe among them, had little use for their properties. Not all the visitors cared much for the social life. One gentleman spent most of his time pent up in his lodgings, playing whist with his landlady and two maids, while Lady Orkney told Lady Harley in 1711 that Bath was a "horrid place", bewailed that she had "not philosophy enough" to bear it, and had not reckoned that "there could be a town in the World without one reasonable creature in it".

One thing, moreover, still stood out. The town was still small (William Penn, in 1704, said that New York was about the same size), and had most of the way to go before proper lodging was provided for its smart visitors. Yet something was done in these first two decades of the new century; the surviving buildings have much interest and pleasing vernacular charm.

As early as 1706 a new Pump Room, in the manner of an orangery with large arched windows, was built for the Corporation by a local mason-builder named John Harvey. Like early Pump Rooms in other spas it was too small and low to be an impressive public building, but the Corinthian columns on the side next the Abbey Churchyard gave it a measure of distinction; one notes that its far nobler successor has its main architectural embellishment on this same side, away from the steamy

corrosion of the King's Bath. In 1708 came the first
Assembly Rooms, with a ballroom added about 1720 by
William Killigrew; from his name it seems that he, like
Ralph Allen, was a Cornish immigrant. Another Bath
designer, Thomas Greenway, had already made his mark
in the charming little riverside building of the Cold
Bath. This had various touches of a Wrennish Baroque,
and like other Bath buildings of this time blended traditional and more contemporary motifs by combining
steep-pitched gables and windows framed by the
swelling "bolection" mouldings much used about 1700.
Some fifteen years later it was Killigrew who designed a
building whose Victorian demolition was a sad architectural tragedy. For the Blue Coat School, ungram-
matically vernacular at a time when Palladian primness
was becoming the fashion, was an impressive building,
with its cupola and with niches set among its windows,
having a touch of the strong character one still admires
in that provincial (and exactly contemporary) masterpiece, the Guildhall at Worcester.

Bath's tally of new streets, in these early days of Beau
Nash, was astonishingly meagre. Trim Street, mostly
woebegone but once important as a new highway of
eighteen lodging houses, was started in 1707 and still has
some "shell-hooded" doorways as well as the pilastered
and pedimented front of the house where Wolfe stayed.
Another "shell" doorway, of great excellence and now
wedged among the display windows of a ladies' dress
shop, is in Green Street, a new highway which led to the
public bowling green north-west of the old city; the
house concerned is largely masked behind the lamination
which produced the shop front, but is dated 1716 in a
gable above windows with bolection frames. Other
windows, in Green Street and in the older Broad Street,
have squared edgings, while broken pediments and
classical pilasters adorn houses in both of these streets,

37

side by side with other features which recalled the Tudor or Jacobean past (plate 7). Some of these rather "traditional" houses may have been built by Killigrew, while Greenway worked more in the idiom of English Baroque when he built, in St. John's Court, four opulent houses whereof one was long the home of Nash. He may also, Mr. Ison thinks, have worked in Abbey Churchyard on the handsome house, with its giant pilasters, built for General Wade who became an important figure in Bath. So too he may have designed its neighbour, with the decorative use of all three classical orders, Doric, Ionic, and Corinthian, which looks back to the Coliseum and Longleat and prefigured the splendours of Bath's Circus.

These early eighteenth-century buildings made up a charming, somewhat disregarded group. Despite early demolitions, and despite sad recent losses in James Street South from bombing and deliberate clearance, they are still worth attention. They shared in the vernacular Baroque tradition which flowered attractively in the house-building of such neighbouring clothing towns as Trowbridge and Bradford-on-Avon, as also in Bristol. House by house they were more entertaining than much of what Bath later witnessed. But one does not feel that these builder-joiners of the Killigrew-Greenway school could have risen to the planning concepts or grand manner of a Wren or a Hawksmoor. How much more exciting Bath could have been had Hawksmoor achieved there such a feat of layout and architecture as he conceived, without results, for the middle of Cambridge. But transport facilities, though envisaged on paper, did not yet exist for Bath's spectacular physical growth. For the moment we turn aside to political excitements.

The Jacobite rising of 1715–16, less romantically remembered than that of "Bonnie Prince Charlie", was really the more important, the more dangerous to the Hanoverians, of the two. Like the Monmouth invasion

14. BAROQUE FROM BRISTOL; Rosewell House, 1735.

15.   Palladian Terrace; Queen Square, North Side.

thirty years before it was planned to break out in several places. As in Monmouth's rebellion serious fighting only flared up in one part of Britain. Yet the western counties, including Bath, were cast for an important role in the upheaval which early threatened King George I.

Bath itself, one gathers, was largely Jacobite in sympathy. A city so much in the Beaufort sphere might be expected to lean that way. Had the second Duke not died in 1714, with the title descending to a boy of seven, the situation in and near Bath might well, in 1715, have been more of a threat to the new dynasty. Even so, Bath was earmarked for a key part in the multiple uprising to enthrone the Prince whose birth, so some claimed, had been aided by his mother's patronage of its waters.

Jacobite feeling in Bath was reinforced by many of its visitors; the government would duly be disturbed by the "concourse of Papists, Non-jurors, and other Disaffected" who converged, in the summer of 1715, on the little city. Sir William Wyndham, the chief Jacobite in the West, arrived and was greeted by vigorous peals of the Abbey bells. So an amusing little counter episode occurred on September 18th, the first anniversary of George I's "happy arrival" in England. Lady Crew, the wife of Lord Crew who was also Bishop of Durham, was at Bath (unsuccessfully as it soon proved) for her health; she lodged with an apothecary in Abbey Churchyard. Despite her close relationship to a leading northern Jacobite now in arms for "James III" she was, to quote the London "Flying Post", "very ingenious and loyal". Upset at the long ringings for Wyndham she summoned the Abbey ringers and bade them peal in honour of the Hanoverian occasion. They replied that there was "mixed company" at Bath, and that some would take offence at prayers for King George. Lady Crew then recorded their refusal in writing, and at her threat of publication the sturdy bellmen thought better of their posture. What they may not have known was that Bath had been chosen as a main centre for Jacobite action, and that it contained quite an arsenal of weapons for use against the new regime.

A rising to overthrow the House of Hanover was actually planned to occur simultaneously near London, in Scotland, in the North of England, and in the West. Of these, the most important move was to be that in the West; the Bath Jacobites openly said that the "effectual attempt" was due there. The Pretender's supporters in Bristol, Gloucester, and Somerset were alerted. Discontent in the clothing districts was stirred up, so that villages which had given Monmouth recruits in 1685 now in 1715 heard bellringings and saw other demonstrations for James II's son. No place was more pivotal than Bath for the insurgents' plans. But suspicions were aroused, and in October, 1715, a month after open rebellion had started in Scotland, the hidden facts were nosed out and revealed.

We are told that Ralph Allen, already at Bath in the postal service, was a leader in this anti-Jacobite movement, and that his political fortunes were largely founded on his loyalty to the Hanoverian winners in the contest. It may well be so, but his name does not feature in the numerous mentions of Bath in the contemporary London newspapers. In any case, there had been indiscreet talk and the authorities in London were aware by now of the dangers that might lurk in the western cities, and in high-Tory Oxford where some Jacobites had incriminating letters from confederates in Bristol and Bath. So troops were sent down to both cities in the Avon valley. The Earl of Berkeley, being Bristol's Lord Lieutenant, did as the first Duke of Beaufort had done in Monmouth's time, secured the city, joined up with the troops, and made some arrests; as Lord Lieutenant of the county of Gloucester he also got promises of immediate action, should the need arise, from the colliers of the Kingswood pits. Lord Windsor's Regiment of Horse, some more cavalry under Col. Pocock, and a regiment of dragoons took charge of Bath; their commander, on this his first contact with a city he would know well in the future, was Major General Wade. It was Col. Pocock who seized what one assumed to have been the Jacobites' chief arms dump in the West. He unearthed eleven chests of carbines, a hogshead full of cartridges, and another of basket hilt swords; the arms were said to be enough for two hundred men. Nor had artillery been forgotten. Three cannon were found, along with moulds to cast more, likewise a mortar. Many horses were seized, arrests were made, and the suspects, like those from Oxford, went under armed guard to London. Wyndham, in the meantime, was also arrested, and nothing came in the West of the Jacobite plans. But the danger, if a little exaggerated, was seen to be genuine. Col. Pocock had felt that Bath was to have been "the rendezvous of the Rebels that were to rise in the West". His regiment was in Somerset for several months to come, for early in 1716 some of his soldiers brawled with a Bruton publican who refused to serve them and damned King and Army alike.* Meanwhile, the Bath magistrates had been sternly rebuked by Lord Stanhope, one of the Secretaries of State, for allowing such a concentration of possible rebels to flourish under their very noses. In October 1715, about the time when Col. Pocock discovered the Bath arsenal, they compliantly replied; among other loyalty-oozing phrases they assured Stanhope that they were "thankfully sensible" of the King's regard in sending Wade with forces strong enough to nip trouble in the bud. They were never to receive any visit from George I. But Wade, in due course, they took very much to their bosom.

* Somerset Quarter Sessions Rolls, County Record Office, Taunton.

The period between the '15 and Bath's great building expansion was that of Defoe's visits. He finished his novel "Moll Flanders" in 1721; though Moll is supposed to know Bath in Charles II's time the conditions described are really those of Defoe's own days, the seamier side of the Nash ascendancy. So Moll makes the tart comment that Bath was "where men find a mistress sometimes, but very rarely look for a wife, and consequently all the particular acquaintances a woman can expect there must have some tendency that way". More openly factual is what Defoe says in his "Tour of England". Some points he makes are widely familiar; he stresses the fact that the habit of *drinking* the waters, as well as bathing, was comparatively new. He acutely notes that Bath's social life was now almost more important than the curative side. He excuses his brevity on Bath's "gallantry and diversions", the best part being "but a barren subject, and the worst part meriting rather a satyr than a description". But on building expansion, for the simple reason that it had not really started, he has nothing to say.

The much needed growth of Bath could not occur before one could assemble on the building sites the whole range of necessary materials. Bath stone, abundant near the city, was easy to bring down by the tramway constructed by Ralph Allen from his Claverton Down quarries to a riverside wharf whence they could go to Bath masons or to destinations elsewhere.* More awkward at first was the transport in bulk of softwood timber for floor joists and roof timbers, of lead, glass, and slates. For such crucial items could only be supplied from the port and industries of Bristol; in the 1720's they could only reach Bath in economic quantities along a

* This important tramway ran down one side of what are now Ralph Allen's Drive and Prior Park Road, and thence by a line once represented by the diagonal alley from Coburg Place towards the river. The wharf, with buildings nearby, is well seen in old prints and maps of Bath.

16.   ARCADIAN VISTA; from Prior Park
(Note Palladian Bridge at bottom)

facing page 42

17. PRIOR PARK;
the Main Portico.

18. PRIOR PARK;
the Mansion Chapel.

river specially canalised for barges. The tramway, and the "navigation" from Bristol, were the two keys to the building of Georgian Bath. Not till *both* problems were solved was the way clear for the architectural achievements of the city we now admire.

Meanwhile, the 1720's saw something of a Wade-Allen ascendancy. Ralph Allen, increasingly wealthy from his system of crossposts, increased his position by his ownership of the quarries on Claverton Down. General Wade, exploiting the advantage gained by routing out the local Jacobites, in 1722 became M.P. for Bath. He soon gave visible proof of his care for the city. For in the sanctuary of the Abbey he installed an opulent marble reredos and richly wrought altar rails in iron. The reredos, so Bristol newspapers tell us, cost him £1500. It was carved by Samuel Tufnell of Westminster; in a classical framing it showed in relief the Adoration of the Magi. This altarpiece has sadly disappeared, but the rails are back in the Abbey, restored from a Lansdown balcony by a generous benefactress. They are now made up into a screen, and their rich scroll and foliate work makes it almost certain that they were forged and wrought by William Edney, the famous Bristol smith. The date of Wade's generosity was 1725, a year also important for the architecture of Bath.

For in the summer of 1725 John Wood, a young surveyor-builder then at work in Yorkshire for Lord Bingley, had sent to him, for his close perusal, the ground plan of the then existing Bath. On the last day of the year he discussed his scheme for the city's future with Dr. Gay, the owner of the gently sloping ground now filled by Queen Square and Gay Street. Wood's schemes, never carried out exactly as he intended, were ambitious, a great advance on previous plans for Bath's expansion. What, then was the precise reason behind this sudden project for "Walcot New Town"?

The navigation of the Avon between Bristol and Bath was an old project, long discussed but not yet a reality. In 1710 a definite scheme was launched; the necessary Act was passed in 1712. The Duke of Beaufort was a leading sponsor. In its preamble the Act clearly admitted that "strangers' resort" was now Bath's main support, and that passenger travel along the Avon would be "commodious and convenient for persons of Quality". Navigation would also help to preserve the highways, would benefit trade, help the poor, and be convenient for the carriage of "free-stone, wood, timber, etc." The Mayor of Bristol was empowered to make the river navigable, and to construct any necessary new cuts and passages. The Commissioners included Westcountry landed aristocrats like Beaufort and Lord Weymouth, likewise a few prominent figures in the Bristol business world.

But many local interests, agriculturalists and colliers among them, were violent enemies of the project. Their opposition, Beaufort's death, and other factors delayed matters for over ten years. When the Act's intention was carried out it was largely thanks to John Hobbs, in business in Bristol as a merchant of softwood timber, shipped into the port from the countries round the Baltic and available for the timberwork of floors and roofs.

In May of 1724 Hobbs started to raise money for the carrying out of the Act. Once this was done Bath could readily be supplied with softwood timber, Welsh slates, iron, and Bristol-made window glass. Bristol pennant stone could also be shipped up in bulk, an important item for it made (and still comprises) the paving of Bath's sidewalks and Parades, an essential amenity for long-skirted ladies when good surfaces in the actual roadways could not be guaranteed. Luxury foods and wines could also be shipped up after arriving in the port of Bristol. Above all came the supply of building materials other than stone. Only when Wood knew that the Act of 1712 was to become a practical reality did he turn his mind to the large-scale expansion of the city. He was only twenty, but his youth did not deter this self-confident young builder.

Wood himself was a strange, in some ways unpleasant character, but none the less a "personality". He was born in 1705, almost certainly in Bath, and sent to the Blue Coat School. His father was a mason, perhaps from Yorkshire. Wood's early building experience lay largely away from Bath, in Yorkshire and in London. He thus learnt his Palladianism, showing little in common with the more vernacular, less classically grammatical builders of the Killigrew–Greenway type who still held the field in Bath. His formal education was slight. His critical powers, whether of himself or other people, were low. He believed, for instance, that the classical orders of architecture had been divinely revealed to the Jews. His ideas both on Bladud's Bath and on that of the Romans were a fantastic farrago of imagination and nonsense. It was fortunate that his technical knowledge ran well ahead of his strictly intellectual training.

For John Wood had had experience on the buildings of a great country estate, and in the swiftly developing Grosvenor-Cavendish area of fashionable London. He did not lack grandeur of ideas. Inspired by his vision of a Roman Bath whose splendours, so he imagined, rivalled Rome itself he hoped to recreate such a city, *fora*, circuses and all, in the neo-Roman manner of his own time. That meant in the disciplined, somewhat bookish Palladian style, itself derived by Palladio from Roman exemplars and now, after a temporary introduction to England by Inigo Jones, the fashionable idiom in high Whig and Hanoverian circles. The mansion of Stourhead in Wiltshire, by Colin Campbell, had already shown the style to the West Country. Now in Bath it was first to appear in a provincial urban setting. In the field of architecture Wood the elder achieved what Nash had done in the social scene, bringing a nationally fashionable, or "London", idiom to dominate a provincial town.

The process was not entirely straightforward, being marred by frustrated schemes, modified details, and unexecuted projects; the reality of the elder Wood's Bath is much smaller, and a good deal more tame, than Wood himself wished. Some of his buildings, moreover, most notably St. Mary's Chapel at one corner of Queen Square, have been destroyed since his time. Nor was it ever true to say that Wood planned a *new city* of Bath, or that Bath's ground plan was wholly revolutionised by his work. What happened, in his time as in later years, was the addition, round the perimeter of the old city, of some piecemeal essays in urban planning and expansion. Not all of these planned areas, before 1754 when Wood the elder died, were that architect's work. Wood's talents were also displayed in various individual buildings, standing separate from the two areas whose present layout is due to him.

An "individual" building was in fact the first in Bath on which Wood actually worked. The income of St. John's Hospital had long been much augmented by the use of some of its buildings as lodgings; being close to the middle of the city, and particularly to the fashionable Cross Bath, the Hospital site was naturally popular with visitors. With an eye to investment the Duke of Chandos had quietly bought much of the Hospital property, and decided to rebuild the residential part of the old almshouses as a dignified courtyard of new dwellings, his own new house being adjacent to the group. John Wood, in 1727, was his eventual choice as architect. Chandos House and the main portion of St. John's court are somewhat cramped and gloomy when compared to Bath's spacious squares and parades, but they were fashionable in their time and the place where Horace Walpole lodged when he came to Bath. The style is the simplest, most elemental Palladian, unadorned and well suited to buildings which would be let as lodgings and would not be the personal possession and pride of aristocratic occupants. But the eastern range (that nearest to the Cross Bath) was planned, in addition to its attractive arcaded cloister, for the reuse of various older ornaments; had these been installed the buildings, which must in their own time have surpassed the general run of Bath lodging houses, would have seemed more ornate and appealing.

The year 1727 also saw Wood at work on large extensions to Allen's fine pedimented house not far from Orange Grove; much of the old bowling green was taken over as its garden, Bathonians being thus deprived of the ground once available for such unsophisticated and rustic diversions as smock racing, pig racing, and eating hot furmety. Beau Nash, one supposes, approved of such changes, while any move that favoured greater sophistication was in tune with what Wood was now actively scheming for Bath's conversion into a city not of rustic Wessex but of Roman-Palladian character.

Wood's vision of Bath was that of a city where several areas would be laid out for the comfortable accommodation and social concourse of fashionable throngs. The Baths and the Pump Room he could not move, and in 1728–30 he added to Bath's stock of centrally placed Assembly Rooms a double cube building for Humphrey Thayer, a London apothecary with large interests in Bath. From its first manageress the suite was known as Mrs. Lindsey's Rooms, and the building disappeared over a century ago. But out on the city's perimeter Wood had his schemes for a whole series of urban agglomerations. One was to be on Dr. Gay's territory at the foot of Lansdown. A second was planned for the Earl of Essex's Bathwick estate. A third was projected for the Pierrepont lands south-east of the old city. Each was to have a "Royal Forum", a "Grand Circus" to recall the Coliseum, and an "Imperial Gymnasium" for (unspecified) "medicinal exercises". Only one of the chosen areas in fact got as far as its Forum (or square) and Circus. No "Imperial Gymnasium", however, has ever graced Walcot New Town, and the Parades are a mere fragment of what Wood first intended for the "Abbey Orchard". In 1726 Lord Essex, being about to marry again, sold his Bathwick property, and that area of Bath had to wait another sixty years for the mere beginnings of a later, ambitious scheme for its high density layout.

John Wood must have spent much of 1727 on his projects for what is now the district of Queen Square. He also did some civil engineering work on the canalisation of the Avon. The job was essentially completed that year; the first barge's cargo, significantly enough, included a consignment of softwood timber. A new cut, had been made at Locksbrook, and over this cut a simple bridge, of the type one associates with Georgian canals and "water-works", is dated 1728 (plate 12). Now at last, with stone brought down from the hills and barges coming regularly from Bristol,* the way was clear. Late in 1728 John Wood, after up and down negotiations with Dr. Gay, and having become the "absolute contractor" for what he planned, cut the first sod of Queen Square. Work continued till 1735. The results were not those first planned, nor does the present Queen Square look like that finished under George II and named to honour his consort Queen Caroline.

* It is worth noticing that Dowry Square at the Bristol Hotwells was started a little earlier than the more ambitious Queen Square in Bath, the factors of production and transport being more favourable at Bristol which had already seen the completion of several brick-built schemes of urban development.

Queen Square, being the local pioneer of such planning ventures, is historically the most important of Bath's urban groupings. Wood intended that the ground should be made level, but the expense was too much. So the square's eastern and western sides, originally meant to answer each other but in fact built differently, slope gently uphill. The southern range, where Wood lived, is a plain Palladian composition of "lodging house" severity. Two doorways, however, are charmingly Baroque; here and elsewhere in this square it would seem, as Mr. Ison suggests, that details were left to local builders not brought up on Palladianism. The western side was attractively rendered as a trio of large and separate Palladian houses, pedimented and with Ionic pilasters flanking their pedimented principal first-floor windows. The rich plasterwork in one of them was perhaps rendered by the Italian Franchini brothers who had also worked in Dublin. The reliefs of Apollo and Marsyas, and of St. Cecilia at her organ, are a particular joy; the rococo exuberance of this stucco work well shows how, in the Palladian period, as distinct from the "Adam" phase of the later eighteenth century, restrained taste in an actual building was by no means always matched in the design of its interior features. The central house on this side of Queen Square was set back from the others, with a large garden in front. The house has long been pulled down, and the front space was filled in 1831 by a Grecian range which long housed a museum, a fine building in itself but out of keeping with the Square's Palladianism and destructive of its original effect. All four of the square's sides were therefore unalike to each other. The finest, built as Wood intended and commanding a southward aspect over the formal garden first filling the central space, was the grand, deliberately palatial Palladian terrace which comprised the northern side (plate 15).

This northern terrace of Queen Square is Bath's most important piece of architecture. Deriving, perhaps, from a somewhat similar terrace in London's Grosvenor Square it gives to a row of separate houses an impression of monumental unity. A set of lodgings becomes a graceful palace. Though it lacks the sculptured frieze such as Wood later placed on his Exchange at Bristol and Town Hall at Liverpool, and though its central pediment would be better for some carving, this terrace has a splendid sense of opulent dignity not belied by such interior features as the staircase and plasterwork of its central house. Corinthian half columns and pilasters grace its facade, the central pediment is capped by rococo urns, while the first floor windows have the little pediments, alternately triangular or segmental, of the Palladian discipline. It was a thousand pities that Wood never had his chance of erecting another such domestic range in Bath. But when in 1740 work started on the Parades, the much reduced fragment of his earlier scheme for the "Abbey Orchard", a fine Corinthian composition planned for the central block in each Parade was omitted, as also were the Venetian windows allowed for the sides. So the North and South Parades, differing somewhat from each other and with many doorways rendered in varied classical designs, are severe and bald. The "Royal Forum" to the South of the South Parade was never built. Even so, as Mrs. Malaprop found, the Parades were a valued addition to Bath's lodging accommodation, and their wide, mud-free promenading spaces of Bristol pennant saved many a brocaded skirt and buckled shoe from spattered ruination.

In a few more years other builders, perhaps Thomas Jelly and William Sainsbury, exploited this conception of the raised and paved Parade in the charmingly secluded, southward-running Gallaway's, or North Parade, Buildings (plate 9). Here too, as was natural in the 1740's,

19. PARTIAL RENOVATION; in the Circus, 1961.

20. SWEEP AND SERENITY; the Royal Crescent, 1767-1775.

Palladian designs were used, and the buildings of this traffic–free *piazzetta* are more interesting than the houses of Wood's Parades. Wood himself, of course, remained active on his buildings down in the city. The most important, commenced in 1738, was the first block of the Mineral Water (originally the General) Hospital. It was part of a widespread movement, in these middle decades of the eighteenth century, to provide hospital accommodation for the general population. It is not one of Bath's more attractive Georgian buildings, but the boldly Ionic treatment of its pedimented main facade made it more impressively monumental than the hospital blocks now built in other provincial cities like Exeter or Bristol. A far grander building of the same period is the great mansion of Prior Park, built by Wood on the prospect-commanding slopes of Claverton Down for Bath's benevolent magnate Ralph Allen.

Allen now felt that his local standing called for a dwelling equivalent to the "stately homes" of the landed aristocracy. Its financial and social background might be that of the self-made businessman turned squire; architecturally it would rank among the great mansions now popular in powerful and blue-blooded Whig circles. His hillside site was superbly chosen. The house, with the flanking wings now fashionable in such country residences, was soberly and grammatically Palladian, entered from behind, and without the neo-Baroque ceremonial stairway which now spills down towards the valley and the dainty Palladian bridge closely copied from that at Wilton. (plate 16)

At Prior Park, with funds amply available, Wood created the greatest of his fairly numerous country houses. Of his interior, little but the columns of the main hall, and the lovely chapel with its coffered apse and two tiers of pillars, Ionic and then Corinthian, survived the fire of 1836 (plate 18). But the main block, though simpler than once proposed, has an exterior very largely as Wood completed it, a great rectangular building of fifteen "elements", with pedimented first floor windows, demure Venetian windows at the sides, an Ionic main feature at the back, and at the front the great six-columned portico, Corinthian with its unfluted columns rather cattily designed by Wood to be just a little larger than those built at Wanstead by Colin Campbell (plate 17). Allen too had an ulterior motive in building so monumental a home. For it was meant as a practical advertisement of the virtues of the Bath stone cut and purveyed by its owner. But Nature long impeded its use beyond the district of Bath and Bristol. Water transport to Bristol and a coaster was easy enough. But a sea journey to London might mean long, storm-bound delays as the ship vainly waited to round Land's End, shooting up the freight charge so that only when the Kennett and Avon canal was open was it economic to bring Bath stone to the capital.

John Wood was not the only Bath builder or architect of this period whose work survives. In Walcot Street, for instance, that thoroughfare now little regarded but in Wood's time of more importance than it is now, a row of houses is dated 1736, while others are in the vernacular manner of the early eighteenth century. A heavily bracketted and rusticated doorway robustly adorns the Bell Inn, while a short terrace of six more has a local builder's version of the Palladian "Venetian" window along all of its first floor. Up in Broad Street the new buildings of the Grammar School were originally to have been built by Wood himself. But the correctly Palladian, nicely pedimented building which was actually started in 1752 was by the busy local mason-designer Thomas Jelly. Its doorway and lower windows are properly pedimented, and the city arms which grace the main pediment show how much better, with such sculptural embellishment, the main building in Queen Square could have been. This school building, the town's best Palladian achievement after Queen Square itself, resembles other Grammar Schools of the time in being essentially domestic in character; like the Hospital it well shows how much more refined and "fashionable" (if a little unexciting) than its opposite numbers elsewhere a Bath building was apt to be.

South of Queen Square, towards Kingsmead and the flat land by the river, a large area was developed by John Hobbs, the Bristol timber merchant whose wares reached Bath at the stone-faced Quay just downstream from the Old Bridge. For his designs Hobbs turned to a Bristol architect, John Strahan, already perhaps responsible for two fine houses which Hobbs had built in Prince Street, Bristol. Now Strahan, as his work in Bath and Bristol testifies, was a fully competent architect, a little vernacular in his idiom and freer than the strict Palladians in his handling of their manner; for that reason he could sometimes be more interesting and characterful than Wood in his more pedestrian moods. Whatever Strahan's standing as an architect he was treated by Wood with jealousy and unworthy spite. Though Wood admitted that Strahan's achievements much exceeded the "common buildings" of other towns he called his architecture "piratical" and declared that only the worse, more "capricious" workmen left his own building jobs for those of the Bristolian. Strahan's work of the 1730's in Bath has much of it perished, and most of his Kingsmead Square is somewhat tame, uninteresting work not unlike that of Wood in the Parades. He is better seen in the charming backwater of Beaufort Square, vernacular Doric in character and with its segmentally pedimented doorways a backward glance, as it were, to the days of Queen Anne (plate 13). His now destroyed Avon Street was somewhat similar, and his work in Monmouth Street was in the same vein. Then in Kingsmead Square Strahan designed a house, for a Bristol client, unlike all others in Bath though with one partial equivalent in Bristol (plate 14). Rosewell House of 1735 has a conventionally Palladian doorway. Its window frames, on the second storey, are of English vernacular character. But it also has strongly Baroque elements. The caryatid herms which flank the main first-floor window, and all the rich carving round the one just above it, are akin to the contemporary decoration on houses in South Germany and Austria. Above four of the first-floor windows are richly carved busts of the widely popular Four Seasons; Bath has them again in the stuccoed corners of a room in a Pierrepont Place dwelling whose heavy Ionic doorway is adorned with carved pineapples, and which housed the musical family of the Linleys. Their fame, like that of Sheridan who boldly eloped with their lovely daughter Elizabeth, lay in the period of our next chapter (plate 10).

21. BRISTOL ROCOCO;
    in the Royal Crescent.

22. NEOCLASSIC;
    in Rivers Street.

GEORGIAN GOTHIC

23. THE HUNTINGDON (now Presbyterian) CHAPEL.

24. In Brock Street.

Chapter VI

THE PEAK IN BUILDING

A S the elder John Wood looked round about 1750
he could gaze with much satisfaction on what he
saw.   His years as Bath's most important architect had
been a time of no mean achievement. He had, it is
true, been unsuccessful with his projects for the improvement of the baths themselves. He had found them
"incrusted with dirt and nastiness" and likened the King's
Bath to "a pit of deformity". But they were still as he
first saw them, and he had had more success on the
ground of private owners than in his relations with the
not very progressive corporate body. He pointedly
contrasts the good condition of the Cold Bath, under
a private owner, with the state of those under the care of
the Corporation. Yet his building of the General Hospital
had been some compensation. He had started, with
many frustrations but also with marked success, on the
expansion of Bath into a Roman-Palladian city. He had
drastically improved the amount and goodness of the
lodgings available for Bath's many visitors. In his "Essay
Towards a Description of Bath" he is most eloquent on
this topic. Before he started work floors in lodging
houses had been browned, to hide the dirt, with a blend
of soot and beer, doors were thin and had inferior locks,
chimneypieces were only of whitewashed stone, and
the furniture was of poor quality by growingly high
Georgian standards. But as houses grew more numerous
their floors, of good deal or Dutch oak, would be

carpetted, and the rooms themselves would be handsomely panelled. Doors were sturdier, staircases (as we can see in Queen Square and elsewhere) would be of excellent joinery, three rails to a tread on their principal flight, while walnut and mahogany (easily bought from Bristol's West India merchants) was normal for furniture. Beds and linen were fit for "gentlemen's capital seats", yet these lodgings, whose servants' garrets were as good as gentlemen's rooms a mere thirty years before, were no higher in price.

Wood himself was respected, a magistrate, and well favoured with commissions, most notably at Liverpool, well away from Bath. He was still in his mid-forties; he could expect to outlive both Nash and Allen, spending several years more on his architectural work. He hoped, in particular, to see new and imposing formal developments in the Walcot area. Work started soon on this aspect of Wood's schemes. The eastern roadway of Queen Square was continued uphill as Gay Street. The houses, on such a slope, had to be "stepped", but no effort was made, by the continuous cornices or platbands later found in Bath, to "unify" the composition. On the eastern side the houses are ended at the bottom by one of attractive design. It is quite unlike its neighbours, with charming, unusually shaped main rooms and heavily rusticated windows. Less acceptable to purists, though pleasing in itself, was the lavish carving and Corinthian pilastering of a house, near the middle of the western side, made famous in Regency days as the last home of Dr. Johnson's old friend Mrs. Piozzi (plate 11). The bottom end of this same block is saved from baldness by well arranged stone panelling and blank windows.

One walks past Gay Street's varied doorways, beckoned on by the great plane trees now dominant, to the ruination of its full architectural effect, in the

Circus which fulfils another aspect of Wood's vision of Bath. Work started early in 1754. Within three months, at the age of forty-nine, its designer was dead. His son, John Wood the younger, born in 1728 and trained, one imagines, more formally than his father, supervised the work and continued the embellishment of Bath. He too was destined to die in his prime, but in twenty-seven years he achieved great things and gave Bath its most grandiose domestic range.

The Circus, always imposing and now regaining much of its early glory of carved stone and ranged three-quarter columns, is on any count a masterpiece. Its interiors vary greatly. The best (and on completion, the most fashionable) are in the segment, so built as to look back towards the sun and a then unaltered country-side of meadow and valley, between Gay and Brock Streets. One other house has its back elevation, and some rooms inside, laid out in the Georgian Gothic manner which is rare in Bath. The exteriors, unlike the doorways in Queen Square and Gay Street, conformed strictly to the overall design of the Woods; the son, it seems, was here a better architectural disciplinarian than his father.

The monumental elevation of the Circus was closely modelled on the design of the Coliseum; "Vespasian's amphitheatre turned outside in", as Matthew Bramble puts it in "Humphrey Clinker", is a shrewd description. Sir John Summerson has also suggested the Place des Victoires in Paris as another source of inspiration. So one has, from the basement upwards, successive tiers of Roman Doric, Ionic, and Corinthian half-columns. Such a blend of the orders is not what the Greeks would have tolerated. But the Romans used it, and theirs was a valid precedent for the Palladians. A much altered parapet has now been crowned again with Bladud's acorns in stone. A frieze of masks and garlands adorns the Corinthian tier, more elaborate than anything in Wood's Queen Square but recalling his Exchange at Bristol. More entertaining, between the triglyphs of the Doric frieze, are the carved metopes with their great range of subjects—heraldry, weapons and mathematical instruments, masonic signs, flowers, fruit and foliage, tragic masks and one human face which Italian friends of mine declared to resemble the countenance of Mussolini (plate 19).

The Circus completed, the younger Wood moved on towards the next of Bath's great formal compositions. The views from the backs of the southern houses of Brock Street were, and are, enchanting, but the street's architecture is modesty itself. Here again the builders varied their doorway designs; not far from the Royal Crescent is one in the "Gothick" linked to the name of Horace Walpole whose Bath visit of 1766 must almost have coincided with its erection (plate 24).

As the Crescent's two ends are rendered, like its circuit, with an imposing giant order of unfluted Ionic three-quarter columns we get, from Brock Street, an intimation of what is coming. But the newcomer has no more than a suspicion of what he will survey as the whole majesty of the younger Wood's masterpiece unfolds. My own first exclamation, nearly twenty years ago, was "Bernini". The Crescent, of course, lies on one side only of the space it embraces. The columns do not reach from ground to cornice, and there are other differences between this great terrace and the colonnades before St. Peter's. Yet there is something in this Bath scene of the sweeping, unadorned majesty of Bernini's colonnades in Rome (plate 20). Though the Crescent's middle is unemphatically marked by two pairs of columns, longer runs of parapet above those pairs, narrow windows on each side of the doorway, and one round-headed window rather taller than its

25.   THE WEIR AND THE PULTENEY BRIDGE.

26. BALDWIN'S GUILDHALL and BRYDON'S EXTENSIONS.

neighbours, there is virtually nothing to give one's eye
a pause. Wood conveyed his æsthetic effect not by
special emphases or by elaboration of detail. His doorways are almost *too* severe, and the Crescent's composition takes one past the Palladians towards the severer
neo-classicism of the Taylor-Chambers school. But as
the Crescent, begun in 1767 and finished in another
eight years, is just old enough to have overlapped with
the dying years of rococo decoration there is, in a fireplace or two and in two ceilings which seem sure to be
by Bristol's rococo plasterworkers,* an element of that
decorative taste (plate 21). In the main, however, the
Crescent's interior features, where individual owners
opted for the rich embellishment of their houses, are
serenely "Adam". Before the Crescent was finished
Robert Adam himself had made his contribution to
Bath's architecture.

The Circus and the Crescent saw Bath well towards
the creation of Walcot New Town. This district, with
Circus and Cresent houses both fashionable and expensive, soon became Bath's "stylish" district. The select
world of hoop skirts and powdered wigs moved up to
lodge on these lower Lansdown slopes. For the waters
they still descended to the Baths and Pump Room. But
for evening junketting it was clearly convenient to have
accommodation much closer than the existing Assembly
suites. After one or two false starts the spacious 'Upper
Rooms", laid out near the Circus by Wood the younger
for a private committee, were started in 1769; work
went swiftly and all was done in a little over two years.
More spacious than its rivals, with rooms fitted up in
the best neo-classic taste, the building provided a large
ballroom, a somewhat smaller tea room, and a noble

---

* They have, for instance, the swirling foliage, and in one case the birds with
necks hanging down from their background, that one finds in Bristol examples
such as the Royal Fort.

octagon for games of cards. All this, bar the fine two-tiered portico, Ionic and Corinthian, at one end of the tea room was bombed to sad obliteration in 1942; the lovely quintet of cut glass chandeliers,* glinting and flashing as they cast their many-hued light, were happily preserved and are among the finest features of the exactly restored interiors; the present rooms are, of course, pleasing reproductions, not originals of 1771. What one does see largely unimpaired is the exterior, somewhat severe as is the outside of many a Georgian country house and no clue to the splendours within. There are however, the first-floor windows, a charming set, pedimented and balustraded below as in Mrs. Piozzi's architecturally eccentric Gay Street house.

The Upper Rooms stood in the midst of the vigorously developed Walcot New Town. The general atmosphere was favourable to such ventures. Bath stood at the peak of its social renown; Nash's death in 1761 had only been an incident, for his glory had long departed and Bath could well manage without him. The Peace of 1763 had ended a successful war; the way for expansion was clear. The main zones were along the London road, in Milsom Street† and from Lansdown Hill towards the Royal Crescent. The houses divide clearly between those built on Corporation land by various local builders, and those erected under Wood the younger's eye on land leased by private owners. The two groups are basically alike, and these areas, with their mainly uniform and somewhat unexciting good taste, and with fronts well drilled by the discipline of the pattern books, give the modern rambler his sense of an overwhelmingly Georgian Bath.

Yet there are some subtle yet readily apparent differences between the groups, the houses laid out under

---

* Of London make, not Waterford as was once thought.
† Its empty site had once been the Rack Close for stretching the Broad Stree weavers' cloth.

Wood's direction being rather tamer than those built by the local plumber cum City councillor Thomas Attwood, better placed than Wood to "muscle in" on the jobs available on "corporate" land. Some of the ranges which were probably his responsibility, Bladud's Buildings for example, Milsom Street of 1761 and the years following, and Edgar's Buildings on its level platform of steps, were built at the same time as the Circus. Others are later, like the gentle crescent of the Paragon, and Belmont high perched on its lofty pavement on one side of Lansdown Hill. All these gain in dignity over the streets in the "Wood" territory by the general presence (except in Milsom Street, Axford's Buildings, and occasionally elsewhere) of pedimented doorways, and of pediments over their central first-floor windows. In Milsom Street and Edgar's Buildings the second-floor windows are more interestingly edged than in Wood's houses or in the others by his competent rival Thomas Attwood.* By contrast, the houses put up under Wood's control have plain horizontal cornices over most of their first-floor windows, and their doorways tend not to be graced by half-columns and pediments but by horizontal cornices on simply rolled brackets; the more decorative doorway of Alfred House is essentially of this design, the urns and the Saxon nkig's bust being additions above the basic scheme. Only in the fine terrace of Alfred's Buildings do we see windows edged in the "Milsom Street' manner, pedimented doorways, a central pediment, and "pavilion" ends to add dignity to the whole. Round the corner in Lansdown Hill one well sees the contrast between these two schools of domestic building. For Oxford Buildings on the western side are in the "Wood" discipline, while Belmont across the way, a more imposing range, is in the "Attwood" manner with a lovely

---

*It may be that some details in these "Attwood" houses were drawn out, in the early 1770's, by Attwood's still abler young assistant, Thomas Baldwin.

curved Adamesque porch added later at the bottom. The "Wood" territory, as one would expect, runs West towards the Crescent, enveloping the Assembly Rooms and stretching up to Rivers Street. One notes the plain facades, without first-floor pediments, in Bennett and Russel Streets, in Rivers Street, and in the quiet, charming little enclosure of Catherine Place, mostly detailed like Bennett and Russel Streets but with its three top-side houses a differing group with Venetian windows to let the southern sun into the first-floor drawing rooms. Doorways, in all these streets of Walcot New Town, are as rewarding a study as in Gay and Brock Streets, for in the more informal setting of a street neither architect could enforce full discipline of outward design on builders or occupants. So here and there, alike in Belmont and in Bennett Streets, and still more in Rivers Street where the prevailing pediments have some charming Adamesque exceptions, a few doorways run counter to the general patterns. So too, in these same quarters of Bath, a few houses, or small streets like the delightful backwater of Miles's Buildings, are unlike their neighbours. Chatham Row, off Walcot Street, is also worth seeing, a sloping terrace of about 1770, most houses being of two elements, but the one at each end having the added distinction of a Venetian window. The best individual house, below Belmont, is Hay Hill Chapel House, very dignified with its pediment, Venetian window, and a rusticated archway enclosing two doors.

One can gain much by the careful perambulation of these "ordinary" areas of Bath. Architectural subtleties apart, plaques on some houses tell of famous residents like Admiral Phillip the founder of Australia, while the smaller plaques of the old Fire Insurance Companies are an added reminder of a byegone social scene. So too, in Milsom and Alfred Streets, are the faded letters, once clear on the masonry, which still announce a Circulating Library and Reading Room (with a State Lottery Office thrown in) and the BATH SELECT LIBRARY whence young ladies like Lydia Languish and Catherine Morland could borrow their "Mistakes of the Heart" and "Mysteries of Udolfo".

This period of great building expansion North of the Avon was also the time of fashionable frequentation and social glory. The spa, with its *macaroni* and its cooks, its preachers and lechers, was an open target for literary satire. It was in 1766, the year before the Crescent was started, that Bath first raved and chuckled over the light but searing satire of Christopher Anstey's "New Bath Guide".* This was also the Bath of Sheridan and Miss Linley, of Gainsborough, of "snug lying" amid the ever accumulating Baroque or neo-classic murals of the Abbey, of Mrs. Malaprop lodging in a North Parade now not quite so fashionable as before. Social Bath, now as in Jane Austen's time, was lucky in the immortality conferred on it by Letters. That stylish life also had results, unexpected but of much interest and lasting value, in the earthier realms of technical and agricultural "improvement".

Edmund Rack, a Norfolk Quaker who shared his East Anglian Christian name with Nelson's father, was the son of a weaver in Attleborough. He became a shopkeeper, being interested also in the well developed agriculture of the "Turnip" Townshend and Coke of Norfolk country. He also a man of literary tastes, and started writing tracts and poems. For this cause, and from a desire for more literary company than the eastern counties could afford, he moved to Bath in 1775. He published a volume of poems, and was soon fortunate in

* The sharp-witted poet, in his passage on old Stucco, who
" has just sent
His plan for a house to be built in the *Crescent* "
shows that he well knew how that building enterprise was undertaken.

his contacts. As Polwhele* puts it, he was "introduced to some respectable personages among the *literati*". Among these were Mrs. Macaulay, and the well-known Lady Miller whose literary sessions out at Batheaston were much ridiculed by Horace Walpole. Residents and visitors alike were of great value to Rack in what now became his main design. He was also helped by contact with fellow Quakers of importance in the business and industrial life of Bristol.

Rack had noticed a great contrast between the agriculture of Norfolk and the backward farming conditions of the West. He believed that Norfolk's lead was largely due to the flourishing Agricultural Society in Norwich. He resolved to start something similar; for such a purpose the socially frequented city of Bath was an ideal base. In 1777 advertisements in the Bath and Bristol papers announced a preliminary meeting, on September 8th, at the famous York House Hotel. Those who came decided to form the Bath Society (soon the Bath and West of England Society), and in another two months the first General Meeting was held. Lady Miller's husband Sir John was Chairman, and the rules were carefully drafted by Rack, who had raised money by many personal visits to the western nobility and gentry. Agriculture was not the Society's only interest. A committee for "mechanic and useful arts" included Wood and Baldwin the architects; another member was the famous Unitarian scientist Joseph Priestley, then at Bowood as librarian to Lord Shelburne. Another committee handled manufactures and commerce; Bristol members included Joseph Fry, the Quaker apothecary and chocolate maker whose interests ranged far beyond medicines and chocolate. The West's textile industries fell naturally into this

* Richard Polwhele, the Devon historian, in a life of Rack in the Introduction to Collinson's *History of Somerset* whose topographical passages were mainly Rack's work.

committee's province. Among its earliest premiums were some for women expert in spinning wool or flax, for improving spinning jennys and cardmaking machines, for better methods of softening water, and for marking sheep without harming their wool with pitch or tar. The Society soon turned to ploughing matches and experimental farming near Bath itself. Its printed Letters and Papers had items by agricultural "improvers" in Somerset, from Arthur Young, and from Rack's East Anglian friends. The Society itself, now best known as the organiser of the "Bath and West", was a good instance of the influence, through a gifted individual, of one part of England on another. As Polwhele said of Rack, "In literature he endeavoured to be useful, in agriculture he was decisively so". Rack stayed on as the Society's secretary till he died, worn out, in 1787.

By the time that the Bath Society had got under way the career of the younger John Wood was nearing its end. His achievement had been considerable; only in the sphere of "public" buildings had he, like his father, largely failed to gain the Corporation's patronage. But late in 1775 the city fathers changed their policy, commissioning him to design the Hot Bath, a pleasing little building with a small Doric portico, most cleverly laid out inside on the basis of a Greek cross. As with all too many buildings in Bath its design has been tampered with, and it does not appear as it did when Wood finished it. Another sphere of Wood's architectural activity was linked to the important matter of the roads round Bath.

The Bath Turnpike Trust* had been set up to improve and repair the main roads around the city. Of these, the London and Bristol roads were the most important.

* Its archives are in the Somerset Record Office at Taunton ; they include superb road maps made in 1786-7 by the surveyor Harcourt Masters, later known as an architect in Bath.

The latter, at this period, was not the present main road over New Bridge, but that which passes through Kelston and so on the Gloucestershire side of the Avon. Its first stretch, with a delightful, sheltered southward view over the broad river valley, was specially esteemed. So a minute of 1757 points out that it was the favoured drive for "persons going to take the air in the cold weather", and that the good repair of such a promenade was of "great consequence" to Bath. From then onwards we often find Wood asked to arrange for the building of Turnpike Houses, and to "settle" their designs before the builders went to work. The records also show that many Bristol businessmen were members of the Trust; one can never escape the importance, for Bath's physical and commercial development, of her larger neighbour. Anstey might sneer that Bristol was only renowned for "commerce and dirt". But Bath could not do without her seaport, and this phase of great expansion well reminds us how vital was Bristol's harbour, with its facilities for timber trans-shipment, for builders in Bath. As one scans the Bristol newspapers for the arrivals and cargoes of ships, one sees how sharp, about 1770, is the rise in timber imports from the Baltic. The connection also had its more cultural side, for it was now that the Bristol and Bath theatres were run together by the postal pioneer John Palmer, with the same piece played at both on alternate nights, and specially fast coaches to run along the turnpike with the cast and their costumes.

Churches and public buildings, some still to be seen, were still put up during these feverishly active years. Early in point of date is the "Gothick" chapel built privately in 1765 by that redoubtable Calvinist leader the Countess of Huntingdon. It stands among the varied houses of the Vineyards, across from the Paragon, and serves now as Bath's Presbyterian church. The rectangular chapel is of no great architectural note, but on

66

27.   ADAMESQUE GRACE; the Guildhall, Banqueting Room.

28.   QUEEN STREET.

its streetward side it is charmingly masked by its manse, a delightful eccentricity (by Bath standards; it would be less unusual in Bristol) with windows and doorways of the ogee shape favoured by "romantic" Gothicists (plate 23). Bathwick Villa, now destroyed, also had many such windows. Another vanished building with Gothic touches was one of the two Anglican churches rebuilt in this period. For St. James', by John Palmer in 1768-69, had an Ionic interior. But the pinnacles, parapets, and outside panelling had Gothic details which owed something, perhaps, to Bristol's churches of St. Nicholas and St. Augustine. The other rebuilt church was that of Walcot, a somewhat dull and boxlike building with pleasing Ionic pilasters, but best seen from the West where its charming little steeple of 1790, Corinthian and then Composite, is capped by a needle-sharp spire.

More important still was the most ambitious and fashionable of Bath's numerous and carefully heated "proprietary" chapels. The Octagon Chapel, off Milsom Street, is the one building in Bath by an architect named Thomas Lightoler who did church work in Liverpool, Manchester, and elsewhere. Internally an octagon, it has a gallery all round, some delicately attractive "Adam" plasterwork, and a small room off its easternmost side which held the Holy Table when the chapel was new in 1767. The Octagon serves now for a variety of secular and cultural purposes; its gallery commanded a better view of proceedings when these were conducted not on the floor of "theatre in the round" but from the loftier vantage point of a two-decker pulpit.

Another, very different "public" building takes us over the river to the lower Lyncombe slopes; the journey is worth making quickly, for the building concerned is derelict and may soon disappear. Up behind the wharf for the shipping of Bath stone, so placed that its pillared verandah had a charming view along a valley not yet slashed across by the railway or filled with numerous buildings, the poor house of the city parishes was started about 1777, a spacious, balanced, attractive building far better than most of its kind; its mutilation and present dereliction is a sad incident in the story of Bath's architectural losses. (*see page* 116).

We come now to the lovely Guildhall, the special glory of genuinely Georgian Bath. The involved story of its building has been very well told by Mr. Ison.* The decision to replace the old pillared Guildhall, on a traffic-free site, was taken not long before George III ascended the throne. In another six years a design by Lightoler, then working on the Octagon, was accepted. But this outside architect was intrigued out of the job by the local, more influential Thomas Attwood. Much controversy then followed, but Attwood's design was actually started, and a fragment of one of its pedimented side wings shows in a water-colour of 1772. But in 1775 Attwood died of an accidental fall. The work devolved on the young Thomas Baldwin whom we have met as Attwood's architectural assistant. In his own buildings Attwood had not deserved badly of Bath, but the city owes him even greater gratitude for the successor who naturally followed him as civic architect (nor only in civic building) in the years which now followed. Wood and Attwood, both belonging in essence to the now declining Palladian school, were less in tune than the neo-classicist Baldwin with this last quarter of the eighteenth century.

Baldwin demolished the beginnings of Attwood's Guildhall, and from 1776 onwards built the stylish neo-classic masterpiece which one now admires as Bath's noblest public building, still blessed with the city's best Georgian interior which is most rightly the heart and centre of the city's frequent musical festivals.

* In pages 35–37 of *The Georgian Buildings of Bath*.

Baldwin's Guildhall is now only the middle block of a larger complex, being shut in on each side by Victorian classic additions, and having a modern dome. Its main front has a central feature whose pediment contains the City arms and is upheld, above good "vermiculated" rustication, by four Ionic half columns. The parapet is still happily crowned by its quartet of Adamesque urns, and the glazing bars which should subdivide such Georgian windows have now been happily replaced (see plate 26). The eastern facade, with a particularly good, shallow-pedimented composition of first floor windows, is also worth seeing. But all pales before the restrained splendour upstairs in the Banquetting Room.

Cream and gold are the key colours of the brilliant interior created by Baldwin and his craftsmen collaborators. Between some of the Corinthian half-columns, and below the longer sections of the exquisite frieze with its rams' heads, anthemia, and urns, the portraits lend extra colour and richness to the scene. Marshal Wade is there, and so is Ralph Allen by William Hoare. Frederick Prince of Wales gave portraits of himself and of Princess Augusta his wife; both are in rococo frames of special splendour. George III and his unattractive Queen Charlotte are seen in the splendour of state robes. The elder Pitt and Lord Camden are both by Hoare. Again by Hoare, smart and dapper with his rapier and white silk waistcoat, is Christopher Anstey. Above the frieze, the wall below the coved ceiling has alternating designs of shallow arches and oval windows, or answering oval designs in delicate plaster. On the room's window side a large fireplace has above it an ornate panel containing Bath's civic arms and their supporters (plate 27). Across the room, above a doorway, is a somewhat cramped little musicians' gallery; Baldwin put one not unlike it in the

Assembly Room of the fine neo-classic Town Hall which he built, in 1806 to 1808, at Devizes.

Two more of Baldwin's buildings, put up in these years of the American war, are in the middle of the city. Northumberland Buildings, of 1778, is the least attractive of his works, tall and four-storeyed, well detailed with its oval plaques and wavy Etruscan moulding, but heavy from the attic storey which rests ponderously on top of its three pediments. Far better, and from the outside more imposing than the Guildhall, are Somersetshire buildings in Milsom Street. They are out of scale with the rest of the street, and except in the middle their modern shops and banks have sadly mutilated the lowermost storey. Yet Baldwin's noble Corinthian composition, with its bowed-out centre and pedimented pavilion ends, is most accomplished and impressive, both in its general effect and in such details as its rams' heads, garlands, and lion masks. Built in 1782, this group clearly marked Baldwin as the most accomplished Bath architect of his time. The central ground floor ceiling has most delicate "Adam" decoration (particularly its charming little group of crossed agricultural implements); it shows that Baldwin's craftsmen served him as well on this private venture as in the civic setting of the Guildhall.

The Bathwick estate, with its floods and mists, had not, since Lord Essex sold it to the Pulteneys, been filled with houses. When let out as gardens its rich soil commanded high rents, while across from Abbey Weir Spring Gardens had become a favoured pleasure resort. The little village had some 250 people when Rack described it for Collinson. The small church, with its "saddleback" West tower, was a humble building; it had a mural to a Skye Highlander, John Mackinnon, "an honest man" who had led the Young Pretender from Culloden field, and then lost the use of his limbs

29. In Bath Street; Curves and Colonnades

30. INSIDE THE PUMP ROOM, 1961.

from lying hidden in the moist bogs as he strove to escape. But one could not ignore the opportunities latent in a large expanse of flat ground—that rare commodity in Bath. In 1768, a prosperous peacetime year, William Johnstone Pulteney first moved in what proved to be a sad sequence of frustrated hopes.

The Pulteney Bridge, with Florence's *Ponte Vecchio* or Palladian precedents in mind, was built in the next few years (plate 25). Its sponsor, at home in the London world of high fashion and taste, employed a "national" architect, and the bridge is Robert Adam's one work in Bath. Its three arches were to lead over to a large district of houses which Adam planned on paper but never saw built. The roadway was flanked not by balustrades but by two rows of dainty little shops. Each side had a central feature and domed and pillared pavilion ends. The bridge is still among the best known and best loved structures in Bath. But except on the downstream side, whose outer face has been restored to the semblance of Adam's many-windowed conception, the Pulteney Bridge is a mere wreck of its first self. Upstream, as one now sees from the Walcot Street car park, an appalling penthouse clings to most of its length; the picture is of desecration and squalor, a noisome disgrace to the beauty of Bath. The four corner pavilions have lost their columns, and though on the southern side some elements remain of Adam's charming little shop fronts, on the other side there is little but a long slab of Victorian plate glass. Adam's drawings show just how the bridge's roadway should look. The full restoration of those shops, as of the upstream face, would be a most worthwhile act of architectural piety.

Pulteney Bridge was meant, of course, to lead to a Pulteney Estate. But nothing happened, for some years, except a city prison. Adam's plans, not surprisingly

where an "official" building was concerned, were
rejected for those of Attwood. His prison, of 1772, is a
dignified pile; since the demolition of London's great
eighteenth-century prisons it is the best building of
this type surviving from Georgian times. Its main
details recall, more monumentally, the composition of
Attwood's domestic ranges.

Bathwick's development then hung fire for several
years. When in 1788 work started on Laura Place, and
on Pulteney Street, built above flood level on its arched
causeway, the architect was Baldwin. The spacious
street, with its octagon vestibule, is good to walk along
and seems Bath's noblest thoroughfare till one studies
its elevations (plate 31). There, however, Baldwin was
well below his best. His Corinthian pilasters seem
"stuck on" to the long facades, at regular intervals but
without real significance. Even the pedimented main
feature of what is now the Cleveland Hotel is faulty
because one sees a row of ten such pilasters where the
great pediment, with its Pulteney arms, needs no more
than six. Better than this composition are the delicate
details of the more important first-floor windows in the
other blocks. But Baldwin's work on this side of the
Avon is more satisfying still in the old village highway
of Bathwick Street, with its serried row of attractive
three-light, pedimented main windows.

By 1790 a new wave of building had set in across the
Avon. The houses mostly climbed up Lansdown or else
were strung out, beyond Walcot church, along the
London road. So hot was the pace that building
became sheer mania, spurred by renewed prosperity
and confidence in these peacetime years between 1783
and 1793. In spas and seaside resorts this general
building rage was specially marked. In Clifton, for
instance, new terrace ranges were started on many
sites of a scenic splendour which not even Bath could

match. Their pennant rubble was now faced, in fashionable imitation, with waterborne Bath stone. In Bath itself new rows of houses arose not merely for visitors, but for the comfort of a growing "residential" population. Designers from outside, including the Bristol architects, were kept at arm's length. The local fraternity, Thomas Baldwin, John Palmer, and John Eveleigh among them, kept the promising market to themselves.

The first building we need notice is among the most attractively planned. It is Portland Place of 1786, reached off Julian Road up the steep Burlington Street which fans out in a triangle to display the whole dignified, simply detailed, reposeful length of the terrace. Its best feature is its basic planning—the dramatic approach and the way in which Portland Place, like Edgar's Buildings across the top of Milsom Street, is raised on a stepped platform so that contours are counteracted and a level site, essential for any classical composition, is obtained. Steps being awkward for chairmen as they lifted their burdens of towel-wrapped, puffing humanity, the middle of this platform is graced by a gently sloping double ramp.

Palmer's work is chiefly seen in the sober, competently neo-classic architecture of St. James's Square and Lansdown Crescent. The square, of the early 1790's, achieves more completely what Wood the elder had hoped to do in Queen Square. For Palmer's eastern and western sides, stepped up the slope and each with its trio of little pediments, correspond to each other. So too, unlike Queen Square, do the shorter ranges on the North and South, both of them attractive elements in this most placidly unspoilt of Bath's squares, bowed out at each end and having central features of four Corinthian pilasters capped by pediments a little too shallow for the full dignity that pediments should convey (plate 35). Bows at each end of the terrace,

73

and a very shallow central pediment, are also seen higher up the hill in Lansdown Crescent, in progress at the same time as St. James's Square and the building by which John Palmer is most happily remembered, serenely poised above the mists and away from the traffic of modern Bath. The order here is Ionic, and the whole essentially classic design must always have seemed ill at ease with the charming Gothic Lansdown Chapel, now destroyed but built by Palmer, a little down the hill, for those who dwelt high perched in this hillside extension of Bath. Along its broad pavement this crescent's full quota of graceful iron lampholders is still there to recall the softly glowing lights which once welcomed the carriages late home from parties and Assemblies (plate 33).

We next look at the geographically dispersed main works of John Eveleigh. He himself was a prosperous builder's merchant who also specialised in the redis-covered mystery of water closets.* He is a strange figure, the odd man out among Bath's late Georgian architects, a curious throwback to Baroque or Palladian, yet not without a touch of genius.

The first of Eveleigh's great compositions was Camden Crescent, begun about 1788 on the eastward-looking Lansdown slopes, serenely regarding the Avon valley and the countryside towards the Wiltshire border. It was started on a steep, treacherous site unsuited for such ambitions; like Lansdown Crescent it loses effect because its one flanking wing runs steeply down hill. The other wing, and much of the main crescent were planned but never finished because landslides made the task too great a risk. What remains is a choice haunt, dignified yet better for its view than for strict architectural quality. The Corinthian pilasters, and the

---

* Sir John Harington and the younger Wood (disastrously) were also pioneers in this sanitary field.

74

31.   Pulteney Street; A Modern View.

32.   Norfolk Crescent, as now restored.

33. LANSDOWN CRESCENT, c.1789–1793.

34. SOMERSET PLACE, c.1791–1793.

central half columns, were made Palladian in the sixty-year old manner of the northern side of Queen Square. The pediment is filled with the arms of Lord Camden; the elephant heads on the keyblocks of the well rusticated doorways are his Pratt family crest. All is pleasingly anachronistic; what one finds less pardonable, by classical standards, are Eveleigh's *five*, not four or six, half-columns beneath his pediment. It is strange, as I know from my own first distant view of Camden Crescent, how physical a shock one gets from such a breach of the Graeco-Roman rules, but the fault is undeniable and hard to explain.

A similar blunder was allowed, about 1791, in another large Eveleigh building. Well out on the London road the simply detailed terrace of Grosvenor curves forward in the middle towards the massive building which started as a hotel; behind it the gardens of a Vauxhall sloped down to the Avon and were to have been flanked by more terraces. The central block is without doubt imposing; despite its *seven* enriched Ionic columns it has much dignity and assurance. Yet here again John Eveleigh produced an architectural anachronism, and his building would look better, and more satisfyingly Baroque in flavour, had the carved plaques, and the garlands on the columns, been finished as first planned. A much better Eveleigh building, with a truly lovely skyline for its main feature, is Somerset Place, secluded on its hillside site past Lansdown Crescent. Minus elephant heads, its rusticated doorways resemble those of Camden Crescent, and like that crescent this terrace remained unfinished. What makes Somerset Place so notable is its great segmental pediment, with carved drapery and *pateræ* of an Adamesque type, but gracefully broken in the middle in a way which would have seemed normal a full century earlier (plate 34).

Palmer and Eveleigh's buildings are the most important of those started during Bath's expansive mania. They were not the full story. Marlborough Buildings somewhat sharply closed the Woods' great sequence from Queen Square to the Crescent. Down in Kingsmead Seymour Street (now wholly demolished) was built, and the first part of the great triangle of Green Park was started. Less well known is the long row, very simple and only marked in the middle by some extra carving on doorway brackets, of Kingsmead Terrace. It must, when new, have had a pleasant dignity; it has since experienced social descent.

Our tour of immediately pre-Napoleonic Bath ends back in the ancient centre, at buildings concerned with Bath's *raison d'être*. It was Thomas Baldwin, as City architect, who rebuilt the Cross Bath, gave Bath its best piece of planning, and started on a spacious new Pump Room for the increasingly thronged morning ceremony of water drinking. The curtain wall of his delightful Cross Bath, Baroque in its sinuosities but wholly neo-classic in its delicate decoration, was the first of these achievements. Then in 1791 he laid out Bath Street between the Cross Bath and one of the beautiful pedimented Ionic colonnades he had built already to flank one end of a new Pump Room. The street, with its little crescents, or *glorietas*, at each end, with its pavements covered and the upper storeys held up by tall Ionic colonnades, is as good a piece of townscape as anything in England. The columns, perhaps, are more slender than strict classical proportions allow, but such dimensions were common in late Georgian as in Hellenistic design, and do not spoil the main effect. A band of graceful Etruscan moulding parts the first and second floors, and the main first floor windows, pedimented in the old Attwood manner, have friezes with a delicate carved decoration of garlands and ribbons (plate 29).

Bath Street brings us close, at its eastern end, to the fine treatment which Baldwin gave, in 1791 or early next year, to one end of his new Pump Room. It has, perhaps, a slight excess of "vermiculated" rustication, but its paired Corinthian columns and blank windows, like the colonnades at each side, are Baldwin at his admirable best. Before he could finish this important public building its architect was at odds with his civic employers, and lost his post in 1792. So the Pump Room was finished by Palmer and he, perhaps, was largely responsible for its dignified facade onto Abbey Churchyard, with its Pindaric quotation in praise of water, and for the noble Corinthian interior whose happiest feature, in the alcove behind Baldwin's end facade, is the beautifully sinuous little gallery which recalls a feature on the Cross Bath (plate 30). The room's general feeling, however, is less of the 1790's than of the Roman neo-classicism seen in some earlier works of these fruitful Bath decades which followed the Crescent's commencement.

The year 1792, which saw Baldwin's dismissal, was a good time for a Bathonian to take stock of his dear city's physical growth. It seemed, as in all quarters he saw starkly white terraces in progress or just finished, that nothing could stop the great property boom which engulfed Bath, like other resorts. There was, indeed, a latent threat from growingly popular Cheltenham, since George III's long sojourn in 1788 an ever more fashionable summer spa. But the atmosphere, despite war and political anguish abroad, was still of complacent hope. This year of wide optimism also saw the peak of the "canal mania", with daily projects whereof few, in the upshot, led to barges gliding softly on still waters. Yet within a twelvemonth all was changed. The Revolution had burst its French bounds, King Louis had gone to the guillotine, two decades of war had started. Financial

77

panic had followed war's outbreak. Many banks had failed, including two at Bath whose collapse dragged Eveleigh and Baldwin into bankruptcy. Building schemes all over the city (as also in Clifton) had come to a halt. Social life, in that untotal conflict, continued apace. But Bath's picture, in 1793, was one of building in suspense.

Chapter VII

REGENCY DECLINE

THOUGH the long war against Napoleon brought
much building to a standstill, many visitors still
patronised Bath, while middle class residents from all
parts came to live in so favoured a city. "Retired"
people, clergy for instance or military men, or Anglo-
Indians home from such places as Masulipatam or
Madras, came to spend their declining days in Bath.
The Reverend Edmund Nelson and the Reverend
George Austen both resided in the city. They could well
have known each other; one can imagine their meetings,
with discussion on the exploits of their naval sons. Social
life, moreover, went on with little interruption; neither
"Northanger Abbey" nor "Persuasion" gives the feeling,
despite competing resorts and the epic conflict of the
Dynasts, that much in Bath had changed.

One point, however, was noticeable,—the way in
which opinions had altered about the regions of Bath in
which it was most fashionable to live. Bathwick, at this
time, was a "good address", but most people rightly felt
that the shut in, enervating districts, lying low in the
misty valley, were to be avoided. The better air of upper
Clifton, as I know from living in both places, was
preferable in Bath's long, drowsy days of high summer
heat. Lady Nelson, one finds from her letters, was
positive on the point. As she wrote to her husband, from
down in New King Street in the spring of 1797, she would
not press an unsettling move to Clifton on her old

father-in-law. But she herself, finding Bath "so hot in the
summer, and so stinking that very few remain in it" was
sure that "a little country air" would do her good.
Finance, however, was an inducement to stay in Kingsmead. For rents in New King Street were only £90 a
year against Gay Street's £160 and still more above that
level; "the higher you go the dearer" was how she put it
to Horatio as he planned the battle in the Canaries which
cost him his right arm. But the Nelsons duly moved, a
little higher than Gay Street, to a house in Bennett Street
close to that occupied, at his death in 1814, by Governor
Phillip who first "settled" Australia. The Nelsons knew
him already, for in April of the year following Horatio,
referring to the Governor as "a good man", asked his
wife to "remember me kindly" to the famous coloniser
and his wife. The year was 1798, the year of The Nile.
The far end of New King Street soon saw new buildings
whose names honoured Nelson and the most tactically
complete of his victories.

The buildings one here encounters are Norfolk Crescent (after Nelson's native county), Nelson Place, and
the short thoroughfare of Nile Street. Nelson Place has
some fine Ionic pilasters at one end, but the main
composition, its watchman's hut still standing sentinel
before it, is the tall, grandiose crescent. It was partly
bombed in 1942, but the gutted gap has lately been well
rebuilt, and made very different inside, as Corporation
flats. Projected before the war of 1793, the crescent was
painfully slow in building, long lay unfinished, and was
only completed after the coming of peace. It has a noble
dignity, sweeping on towards the river and so placed
that it must once have had a charming, though often
misty, view. But something is wrong in the middle. Four
Ionic pilasters and a pediment are there to make a
centrepiece. The unknown designer avoided Baldwin's
bétise in Northumberland Buildings, for his attic storey

does not crush down on his pediment. But a whole storeh of windows has very oddly been allowed between the pilaster capitals and the shallow pediment above. It would seem, from such expedients, that four main storeys are one too many for the best effect of a classical terrace.

Despite the long war, Bath's building activity did not wholly cease. There was, indeed, much need for new housing. Bath's population, in the first census in 1801, came out at over 32,200 for the urban area,* thus making the city the ninth largest in England. Not all Bath's continued expansion had to await the cease-fire which in 1814 sent Napoleon to Elba and the likes of Captain Wentworth ashore to the young ladies in Bath. But unlike Cheltenham, Bath does not give the feeling of a mainly Regency or Greek Revival town.

We can first look at some tall terraces, of the war years or just later, which were all designed by the elder John Pinch, a Bath architect of some note. The first is New Sydney Place, of 1804 to 1808. This was one terrace of the eight planned to surround Sydney Gardens, another "Vauxhall" whose dignified, porticoed hotel block had already been built to Harcourt Masters' designs; it is now, much altered since 1918, the Holburne Museum, standing finely as a terminal to the now treeless vista along Pulteney Street (plate 31). New Sydney Place itself is a little unhappy in the placing of its three pediments above the walling and windows of the attics which were now allowed to share in the main frontage without being tucked behind parapets, pediments, or balustrades. It runs up a slope, and unlike earlier compositions so sited, New Sydney Place has each house carefully linked to its neighbour by the curvature of such

* This is the combined total for the parishes of the Abbey, St. James, and St. Michael, for Walcot (the most populous), Bathwick, and Lyncombe-Widcombe. This first census was considerably evaded, so the true total was probably higher. For Bath's relative position, see W. G. Hoskins, *Local History in England*, 1959, p. 178.

features as cornices, string courses, or even the continuous band of Etruscan moulding which forms part of its sparing, delicate decoration. This studied "unifying" of sloping terraces now became common in Bath. One finds it, for instance, in Raby Place at the foot of Bathwick Hill, in early Victorian Charlotte Street, and most dramatically in St. Mary's Buildings off the lowermost stretch of the Wells Road (plate 38).

Above St. James's Square, at first approached by one of the little streets which lead diagonally from its corners, the tall, sloping terrace of Cavendish Place was started about 1808. It has no pediments, but much else in its design is like that of New Sydney Place, and it is in Pinch's most grandiose manner. A little above it the starkly simple, dignified Cavendish Crescent was not finished for nearly twenty years; it is of four storeys and is rather too lofty for its length. Last and latest of these terraces by the elder Pinch, serene and secluded in a delightful part of Lansdown, Sion Hill Place is clearly in its architect's manner, with a small central pediment and pavilion ends boldly bowed towards its level pavement (plate 36).

The grand manner, but not perhaps by Pinch, appears again in the later portion of Green Park, tall and massive and with its finely composed main section so clearly meant to be a central block that one suspects the owners to have intended a new balancing wing, demolishing the earlier houses so as to give these slightly recessed and pedimented windows their artistic due. Across the Avon, in Lyncombe-Widcombe which now became a serious building target, Widcombe Crescent and Terrace, of about 1805 by Harcourt Masters, are delightfully placed off Widcombe Hill. The crescent, like some in Clifton, has its view, and the best rooms, on its convex back side. The ornament, however, is all on the concave façade, very sparing in the manner of its time, but charming

35. St. James's Square, by John Palmer, North Side.

36. Sion Hill Place.

37. REGENCY CRESCENT; CAVENDISH CRESCENT.

38. CLIMBING TERRACE; St. Mary's Buildings.

where the pairs of doorways, set in shallow recessed arches, each have the resulting blank space tricked out with a large rosette and a pattern of festoons. Widcombe Terrace is remarkable in Bath in that *one end*, not its principal façade, is what one is meant to admire, a pair of rounded bows being closely spaced, with a band of Etruscan moulding and a fine trio of gadrooned urns above their parapet. The façade displays its windows, triply divided in the Regency manner and set in the shallowest of arches, to the valley below. Some steps keep wheeled traffic from its quiet pavement, and all is unspoilt and delectable for the gentle drowsing away of a softly sunny afternoon. Lower down in the valley the pedimented terrace of Prior Park Buildings is a little grim and heavy, but as one looks along it a delicious, unsuspected surprise comes from a clearly running little millstream which was made a watercourse between the terrace's pavement and the lawn which parts it from the busy road (plate 43).

Near the foot of Widcombe Hill the Kennett and Avon Canal strikes off from the Avon, starting its long run to the Thames basin in a picturesque sequence of basins, bridges, and quickly succeeding locks. Bath's second port area grew up where barges were gathered on their course, with mean rows of houses and the bulky, well sited "churchwarden" Gothic Ebenezer Chapel of 1821 to serve those concerned with this new "navigation". The canal itself, with Rennie its engineer and the supervisor of its works and buildings, had been long under construction, with controversy and barbed witticisms as work slowly proceeded. Though its authorising Act had been passed in 1794 the canal was only finished in 1810. It became important both for passengers and freight. Now at last the transport of Bath stone to London became economic; what hampered its use was not expense but the mordant grime of the capital.

The towpath, by a well loved, delightful stretch, soon leads to Bathwick Hill, then past it to the short tunnel, below the Warminster road, where Cleveland House rises picturesquely above the cavernous arch (plate 39). The Regency and the two following decades saw much building up Bathwick Hill, with an excellent Grecian composition in Darlington Place whose Ionic main feature looks crossways down its road approach. Below it, St. Mary's which now replaced Bathwick's ancient little church was one of Bath's excellent "pre-Tractarian" Gothic group.

Early in the nineteenth century an architect had usually to be "bilingual", in classic or Gothic, according to his patrons' tastes. John Pinch and his namesake son were well aware of this bread and butter truth. In his terraces and in the United Hospital the elder Pinch was a classic. But when in 1814 he came to design the new Bathwick church he worked, especially in his truly beautiful panelled and pinnacled tower, in Perpendicular not unlike that of Bath Abbey. His whole West end is brilliantly successful and essentially "correct" surprisingly so when one recalls its early placing in the "academic" Gothic Revival (plate 44). The clerestoried nave, as completed with its galleries, plaster vaulting, horizontal beams instead of arches, and tiny sanctuary, was more obviously of its time. After Pinch's death in 1827 his son designed effectively, and even more in the Somerset manner, in St. Saviour's, Larkhall which was started in 1829, as at Bathwick with the stubbiest of sanctuaries. Its architect was also the rebuilder, in reasonably correct Perpendicular, of the nave and chancel at Weston, too bulky for the surviving tower but adequate in themselves; he also worked, in the same decade of the 1830's, on replacement commissions a few miles away at Midsomer Norton and Paulton. We ourselves return to Bath's older districts for other, and earlier specimens of the Gothic Revival's first phase.

The wave of Gothic church building had started in 1798, with Christ Church, Walcot by Palmer (working somewhat in the vein of Lansdown Chapel), a "Free Church" meant largely for the poor who dwelt thickly in the steep little streets of late Georgian "artisan housing" above the level of Rivers Street. The prime mover was Charles Daubeney, the son of a rich Bristol merchant, Fellow of Winchester, later the Archdeacon of Salisbury, and the church's first parson. The building, with many altered windows and a painful Victorian sanctuary, is less regarded than it deserves. Its exterior, less ornate on the side away from the street, has little shields on part of its battlemented parapet, and pleasant grotesques which include gryphons and a playful pair of squirrels. Inside, the clustered pillars and horizontal cornices above them could have given Pinch ideas for Bathwick, while over the nave the main bosses are heraldic and feature the See of Canterbury, the Somerset diocese, and the City of Bath; they would be better were they properly coloured.

The Kingsmead area got another "free seating" church for its poor inhabitants when Holy Trinity was finished in 1822; its bombed ruins only lately disappeared and even in desolation were rare and striking. For John Lowder the architect, having first made a classical design which was rejected, even in these pre-Pugin days, as being inadequately "ecclesiastical", then produced a flamboyant fantasy, with a panelled aisle wall on the more visible side, rich tracery, and a spired corner turret, whose spirit was neither that of the Georgians nor of the Victorian ecclesiologists. Holy Trinity, a sad loss, was a fanciful, little appreciated delight. In a similar vein, romance and fantasy were apparent in the new church at Combe Down, of 1832 and by H. E. Goodridge, the most talented and versatile of the many architects now in Bath. Later generations made it wider and gave it a clerestory. But the tower and spire, with delightfully flamboyant touches by a designer whose Gothic was usually plain Early English, are well worth a visit to these upland outskirts. Not far away, at Prior Park which Bishop Baines now ran as a Catholic College, it was Goodridge, about 1834, who laid out the nobly sweeping processional stairway before the mansion. The real inspiration, one suspects, was less from Goodridge himself than from the famous Spanish Steps in Papal Rome. So too, Beckford's Tower, built in 1826–27 by the erstwhile owner of Fonthill who had now retired to his pair of Lansdown houses, is probably less due to Goodridge than to the insistence of its eccentric owner; its tall, slim fabric is capped, like St. Pancras steeple in London, by a version of Lysicrates' choragic monument at Athens. Turning back to Anglican churches the most beautiful of those started in the 1830's is the new St. Michael's. G. P. Manners its architect had been uninspiringly Perpendicular in St. Mark's of 1832, newly built amid mediocre late Regency terraces in the shadow of Beechen Cliff. In St. Michael's his lovely design is the Early English of Salisbury Cathedral. The trios of lancets and the stepped offsets on the buttresses are clearly inspired from that quarter, while the general interior feeling, despite a small apse and a lack of dark marble shafts, is that of Salisbury's Lady Chapel and retrochoir. But the steeple, tied by no thirteenth-century original on the Wiltshire Avon, is more Manners's own with its spire lightly poised on a crown of little arches, a gracefully pleasing composition, from whichever angle it is viewed (plate 7).

For more proprietary chapels built by Anglicans, and for Nonconformist churches, we go back in time, and return to Bath's prevalent classical tradition. Of the later proprietary chapels the one survivor (now a furniture store) is that of Kensington, completed in 1795 and set conspicuously among the simple terraces stretching out along the London road. The architect was Palmer; his

39. AQUATIC UNDERPASS; The Canal and Cleveland House.

40. PAIRED VILLAS; Claremont Place, 1817.

broad, pedimented façade is well composed with shallow arches and small Ionic pilasters. About the same time Palmer also designed the new Unitarian chapel, simple but competent, much altered now and with its stylistic effect not on a façade but along one side. More monumental, near Walcot Church, was the Methodists' Walcot Chapel. Outside, the façade is all that matters, but that front, by a London architect named William Jenkins, is dignified and effective despite some coarseness of detail and loose architectural grammar. A "Grecian" Doric porch has above it a good row of windows and Corinthian pilasters, while high in the pediment the date 1815 is that of Waterloo. The chapel well shows how the Methodists, not long after their separate denominational identity, took greater care over their chapels' style and dignity. The galleried interior of Walcot Chapel is also of some note, and well suited to "auditory" needs; behind the pulpit the recess for the organ is well flanked by Ionic pilasters and surmounted by a rich plaster frieze. Further on in Walcot is a chapel in Thomas Street, dated 1830 and well composed with its pattern of windows, platbands, and a Tuscan porch (plate 42). It is hardly known to Bath's residents or visitors, being tucked away up a street of incredible steepness which leads up to the charming little late Regency groups, politically named after a prominent Tory Lord Chancellor, of Lyndhurst Terrace and Lyndhurst Place. Nor are these the only Regency chapels in Bath to be worth a glance. Up on Combe Down, near the church and among varied houses of about its own date the Union Chapel, like that of Walcot, was built in Waterloo year. Away on Bath's other extremity the plain Larkhall chapel, very typical of many humble Methodist chapels of about 1820, was built to serve those who dwelt in the "artisan" houses nearby, in the larger terraces of this little visited part of Bath, or in the still delectable backwater of Daffords'

Place whose houses nestle cosily behind the gardens often found, in this period, *in front of* terraces.

The middle of the city is the district for "public buildings" of the Greek Revival. Union, York, and New Bond Streets, both familiar and important in Bath's configuration, were also opened out in these early years of the nineteenth century. Neat little Regency shop fronts also started to encroach on the lower end of Milsom Street, forerunners, in Jane Austen's time, of the dire artistic murder which the Victorians wrought. So too, in the manner of Bristol's splendid double arcade, we find Goodridge's admirable "Corridor". It was built, in 1825, for covered shopping; its chaste, well composed Grecian eastern entrance is across High Street from the Guildhall.

The Bath Theatre had never been well housed in the eighteenth century, and since 1766 its building had lagged far behind Bristol's Theatre Royal. So in 1802 a new, spacious, and splendid theatre was projected. Work started in 1804, and Bath's Theatre Royal was opened nine days before Trafalgar. It fills one side of Beaufort Square, was first entered from that direction, and on that side displays a monumental façade which is much taller than the houses and somewhat dominates the intimate little enclosure. But its design, by the younger George Dance of London and put up by Palmer, is of a compensating dignity. Above six shallow pilasters a frieze of garlands and tragic masks is highly appropriate, while against the skyline the builders put George III's arms and a row of four Grecian lyres. The interior was gutted in 1862. The reopening, in a recreated setting of charm and character, was in the year following, the young Ellen Terry appearing in the chosen play. Thick soot and grime now deface the northern frieze, and none of the four lyres is intact. Cleaning and restoration, as is now being done in the Circus, would be an overdue yet welcome improvement to one of Bath's notable buildings, a rarity among our theatres in having a *side* elevation which is meant to be seen and admired.

Likewise by an outsider were two Bath buildings by William Wilkins, a "bilingual" architect first famous as a national leader of the academic Greek Revival. In 1806 came the portico added, not long before their complete rebuilding, to the Lower Rooms. That year Wilkins published his "Antiquities of Magna Graecia", a book of much influence for the course of the Greek Revival. The portico, Greek Doric and fittingly copied not from Athens but from the latest and most sophisticated of the three temples at Paestum, thus came early in the Revival and a year before Wilkins started his Athenian Ionic Downing College at Cambridge. The Rooms themselves, soon after being the scene of Mrs Piozzi's great party on her eightieth birthday, were burnt out in 1820. Rebuilt, behind Wilkins' portico, they long housed Bath's Literary and Scientific Institution, their Grecian style being thought fitting for the Athenaeums and Institutions now founded all over the country. Nearby, in the meantime, the Masons had employed Wilkins to design a new hall started in 1817; it is now the Quakers' Meeting House. Its portico, of two columns *in antis*, is pure Athenian Ionic, well showing the Greek Revival, at its most correct, by a leading exponent (plate 41). Ionic again is Partis College whose fine three-sided court of 1825–1827 overlooks the Avon valley from the old Bristol road. The word "College" need have no educational meaning. It is really a "gathering together" of people for any particular purpose. Here on Bath's outskirts (as in Salisbury's lovely College of Matrons) that purpose, as laid down in his will by the Rev. Fletcher Partis, was to help "reduced gentlewomen". The building, among Bath's best of its time, was by Samuel and Philip Flood Page, two otherwise obscure architects from London. In the middle of the court's long side a portico leads to the chapel. The whole admirable grouping has a feeling of Downing College's upper end as finished in the 1950's, and as one of Wilkins's unsuccessful competitors designed it.

Soon after the building of Partis College came the time of Dickens's visit to the starchy, affected Bath of Angelo Cyrus Bantam, of whist-crazed dowagers in ambush for Mr. Pickwick behind their tables in the Upper Rooms, of comic nocturnal adventures along the Royal Crescent. The most immortal of Dickens characters got his name from Bath, for Eleazer Pickwick, of a well-known local family which must have come to the city from the hamlet of Pickwick near Corsham, was landlord of the White Hart where Dickens makes his hero and their party stay on their arrival. In his pages one still sees the Bath of transient visitors, but the 1830's were also the time for ever more permanent residents. So individual or "paired" villas, not so good as at Cheltenham but numerous, important, and mostly "Grecian", grew up on the fringes and along the coach roads. One finds them in Upper East Hayes, up Bathwick Hill, and along the road to Bathampton. Claremont Place, dated 1817, is an excellent quartet of the "semi-detached" (plate 40), their central wallspaces filled for artistry's sake with blank windows whose masonry was at first painted black with a white pattern of glazing bars; the same device was exploited in Cambridge Place up Widcombe Hill. A group of Gothic villas is in Entry Hill as one descends from Combe Down. Others, occasionally with such embellishments as pilasters, are along the road to Weston, and a particularly tasteful house of this type is the vicarage at Weston itself.

Nor should one forget, in this context of lasting residence, the many rows of smaller houses tucked away among Bath's outer fringes, humble enough when built

41. MARSHAL WADE's HOUSE, Abbey Churchyard, circa 1720.

42. (*Top Left*)
"Regency" Contrasts
Prior Park Buildings
—Classical.

43. (*Top Right*)
St. Mary's Bathwick
—Gothic.

44. (*Right*)
Masonic Hall (now
Quakers' Meeting House),
by Wilkins, 1817.

but of a size which nowadays one can happily inhabit, as one unit, without the harsh subdivision which has befallen most houses in the larger, more stately terraces. We may find them in Lyndhurst Terrace and Dafford's Place which I have mentioned already; Sydney Buildings in Bathwick, above the canal and with its gardens running down to the weedy water, is another row of such houses. So too, up Lansdown, is the simple Regency terrace of Richmond Hill. The Lyncombe-Widcombe district is specially full of them, for its growth in population was now relatively greater than elsewhere in Bath. Devonshire Buildings and other terraces of this period are in the region of Bear Flat, while up Lyncombe Hill many houses of this modest type lie above the grim Regency grouping of Southcot Place. Oxford Terrace, to one side of this steep road, seems likely, with its central pediment, to be by the builder of Camden Place not far past Camden Crescent, while other houses on this Lyncombe height lie charmingly behind good ironwork or at the head of their gardens. The actual roads, like some others in Bath, are still apt to be lit by the Regency lamp posts put up when in 1819 gas lighting first shone upon the city. These roadways are happily quiet and secluded as one lingers among their small houses, delightful little eschato-Georgian bijou residences, worth noting in their secluded, scarce-known charm as they nestle on their view-commanding heights behind flowery little front gardens shut in by their cat-capped walls.

Chapter VIII

VICTORIAN VARIATIONS

THE fictional Bath of Mr. Pickwick was also the
Bath of the stage coach, and a scene of activity for
that very real, practical personality the elder John
Loudon McAdam. For he, who since 1815 had been
surveyor of the Bristol Turnpike Trust, from 1826 held
the equivalent post under the Bath Trustees. These last
few years before the railway saw great improvements
in the roads round Bath, and the city was fully caught
up in the second phase of the Transport Revolution.
It thus saw a great increase in its vehicular bridges
across the Avon.

The first of these bridges, between Bathwick and
Walcot, was Goodridge's Cleveland Bridge, an iron-
girdered, single-arch creation of 1827. It has been
rebuilt this century, but at both ends it is still adorned
by its delightful quartet of Greek Doric tollgatherers'
lodges. Its Walcot approach gave Goodridge his chance
to create Cleveland Place, an excellent, spacious piece
of planning whose houses have linear detail in the
manner of Soane. Then in 1835 North Parade ceased
to be a *cul de sac* when North Parade Bridge was started
by Tierney Clark, the London civil engineer who built
the first Hammersmith Bridge. Here too the actual
arch has been rebuilt, but on each side the imposingly
rusticated masonry piers are the originals. Lower down
the river, in an area now dingily industrial, the Victoria
Suspension Bridge was opened in 1836 and took its

name, like Bath's attractive Victoria Park and a well known street in Clifton, from the heir presumptive, not yet Queen; its simple arched pylons are good essays in the Grecian manner still fashionable for such structures. Grecian again, lower down and carrying what was now the more important of the roads to Bristol, is the beautifully cycloidal New Bridge as widened and re-fashioned between 1831 and 1834. A graceful single arch, with approaching causeways, had comprised this bridge when Collinson's picture of Kelston was made about 1790. Now however, with more wheeled traffic and the present Newbridge Road a more convenient highway to avoid the severe gradient of Old Newbridge Hill, it became necessary to improve it. The Turnpike Trustees called for plans from Goodridge, William Armstrong of Bristol, and a London architect named George Smith. Designs by Armstrong were eventually accepted and his, æsthetically speaking, is the fine bridge we now see, with severe Grecian panelling on its piers and bold rustication to edge its arch. But one notes, from below, that the bridge is not new but widened, while arches and rough pennant masonry from the older approaches are conspicuous within some of the more numerous causeway arches of Armstrong's construction.

The coming of the Great Western Railway was what really swept Bath into modernity. The great event was on August 31st 1840, when the twelve-mile section between Bristol and Bath was opened with a service of ten trains each way on weekdays, and on Sundays of four. The single fare was half a crown first class and 1s. 6d. in the second. Bells and cannon marked the day of inauguration, and vast crowds watched the scene. Twenty trips, on that special day, were run each way; many passengers travelled for no lasting reasons, but just for the experience. Four engines were available, and the first-class carriages were styled "somniferous" by some Bristol journalist. Not till June, 1841, with the Box Tunnel completed, was the whole line open from Paddington to Bristol; only on the actual opening day were all the works finished near Bath. Brunel's station, still displaying its neo-Elizabethan façade, lost its main feature when its great single-span roof was pulled down. Along most of the Bath section, and most notably just West of the station and at Twerton tunnel, the stylistic note is Perpendicular or castellated. But the splendid brick bridge at the end of Pulteney Road is Brunel at his best with its diagonal alignment, bold parapet, and shallow elliptical arch. Classicism was well respected in Sydney Park, and in the easterly Avon bridge there is some curiously individual Baroque (plate 45).

The railway led naturally to growth in Bath's industry. In size and population the city expanded, the 66,886 people of 1901 being nearly double those of a century before. The old centre slowly declined, the large increases being in Weston, over the river in Lyncombe-Widcombe, and in markedly industrial Twerton. It was here that clothmaking continued on "factory" lines. Several mills were built, and that once used for other purposes by Messrs. Cook was a very good piece of industrial architecture of about 1850; its pavilion ends with their lunettes, its unusual corbels, and the goodness of its masonry all made it worth attention. Printing became a major Bath industry. So too did engineering, and about 1875 Stothert's foundry, long in business and the maker of some charming little Regency bridges over the canal, moved to the larger site where the works, with cranes as their best known but by no means their only product, are now famous as Stothert and Pitt's. The river, despite the railway's competition, was still much navigated. We even hear of shipbuilding in Bath, a few seagoing craft being launched there between 1840 and 1847.*

Nearly thirty years after the Great Western the Midland Railway reached Bath from Gloucester via Mangotsfield. Its station of 1869 was far better than Brunel's, being spanned by iron girders like a miniature St. Pancras, but beautifully fronted not in polychrome Gothic but by a most chaste and dignified forebuilding whose style paid sensitive respect to Bath's dominant traditions.

Bath's early Victorian classicism was partly Ionic of the Greek Revival. The style was found, off Manvers Street, in the graceful little Swedenborgian church of 1844. A year later Goodridge's dignified Dispensary adorned one side of his existing Cleveland Place. Roman or Renaissance trends could also, however, be seen. In 1844 J. J. Scoles designed a splendid basilican church for the Catholic College at Prior Park, barrel-vaulted, with fluted Corinthian columns (finished in the 1880's) and a stately pillared apse; it may have been inspired by the upper stage of the chapel at Versailles. In 1845 James Wilson, a prosperous architect important in Victorian Bath and much employed elsewhere, built the new Moravian (now Christian Science) chapel in Charlotte Street; he gave it a comanding, success-ful Corinthian portico whose four columns are not evenly spaced as the Greeks would have had them but are arranged in two pairs. Next door in this interest-ing street the Savings Bank had already, in 1841, been designed by George Alexander; it is a chaste and beautifully composed essay in the Italian Renaissance manner made famous in the great London clubs.†

Then in 1848 the English Renaissance tradition of Wren

* See Grahame Farr in Somerset Archæological Society (Bath and District Branch), *Proceedings*, 1939–47, p. 79.

† It is now Bath's Register Office.

or Gibbs was well shown, by Manners and Gill, in the fine steeple of St. James's church which outlasted the bombing till its demolition in the 1950's.

Less happy, in the early 1840's, was Bath's experience of neo-Romanesque; of all mediæval styles this was surely the least happy when "revived". Bath's specimens are luckily unobtrusive—the Irvingite church (now a Roman Catholic hall) by Manners and Gill and a small cemetery chapel in Walcot are two examples. Another, more prominent, is the remarkable railing along the high pavement, and down its steps, in George Street. The best, with a tower to give it dignity, was Manners's chapel of 1843 in the new, attractively laid out Abbey cemetery in Lyncombe. Far worse was the move from "Norman" to Byzantino-Lombard. Below Beckford's Tower the cemetery gateway is a late work by H. E. Goodridge, elaborate and a sad fall from his earlier standards. Another horror, adding interest to Charlotte Street but not embellishing it, was the Percy Congregational Chapel on which Goodridge and his son collaborated in 1854. It is octagonal with a turretted, much arcaded façade; one almost feels that Ravenna's S. Vitale had mated with some Lombard basilica some six centuries less old.

Bath's other Victorian places of worship are inflexibly Gothic. St. Stephen's up Lansdown, by Wilson though later enlarged, was started in 1840—early enough for its plan to be in the "pre-ecclesiological" tradition. Its tower, with an unusual lantern of romantically fascinating design, looks delightful whether seen from afar or up the last stretch of its roadward approach. Very different, of 1846–47, is Manners and Gill's church of St. Matthew, a strictly ecclesiological, pseudo-Decorated building with its tower and spire well sited at the foot of Widcombe Hill. Except for some fancifully transomed main windows it is not unlike the same architects'

St. Paul's at Tiverton. The only Victorian architectural giant to design a whole church in Bath was Sir Gilbert Scott (responsible also for the final restoration of the Abbey and the sympathetic fan vaulting of its nave). St. Andrew's, behind the Royal Crescent was built early in the 1870's, a reasonable achievement in the East Midland Early English so beloved of Victorian church architects but on all counts an exotic in its Bath setting. It was bombed in 1942, and with its steeple now demolished the eastward view along the Crescent is no longer sullied by its intrusion (plate 20).

The Roman Catholics built two churches in Bath. St. John's, a strange neighbour for the Palladian South Parade, was by the prolific C. F. Hansom. Its tower and spire are excellent Lincolnshire Geometrical, but the apsed body of the church, with its pink granite and spindly ironwork, is unworthy of its steeple. St. Mary's in Julian Road, of the 1880's, is ornate, quite interesting Decorated and still lacks its western end. Bath's other Victorian churches, of all denominations, one can leave in the silence of æsthetic contempt. The Gothic cemetery chapels are really more rewarding, particularly one in the Roman Catholic cemetery, the two (Early English and octagonal Decorated) in St Michael's cemetery, and C. E. Davis' beautiful pair of 1862, with a shrine-like central spire, in the cemetery off the drab highway of Lower Bristol Road. Gothic buildings of a more imposing type are two contrasting schools by Wilson. The first block of Kingswood, completed in 1851 when that Methodist School moved in from its old quarters at Kingswood near Bristol, is a balanced, formal composition, essentially classic but in Gothic dress. It is, in fact, a slightly more ornamented version of the buildings which Wilson had erected, between 1841 and 1843, for Cheltenham College. Less regular in its planning and more in tune with most Victorian Gothic of 1853

97

when it was built, was the towered, many-gabled range which first housed a boys' school but soon became, and remains, the Royal School for Army officers' daughters.

As in the Midland Station, it was in various secular buildings that Bath's classical character was most sturdily maintained. Banks and modern shop fronts stayed squarely within the traditions of classicism and the Renaissance. When in 1869 the ponderous pile of the Grand Pump Room Hotel replaced the Pickwicks' White Hart the building, though large for its surroundings and more akin to the French seventeenth century than to Georgian Bath, was at all events Corinthian classical. In Broad Street the Y.M.C.A. building of 1887 was given a very reasonable Victorian classic frontage. More important, and so sited that they are much seen and well known, are the buildings by the London architect J. M. Brydon.

Between 1893 and the end of the century Brydon was busy on some important civic commissions. The opening up of the Roman Baths required a dignified classic setting for the newly visible remains. The Great Bath's colonnade and its statues were thus followed by Brydon's eastward enlargement of the Pump Room. The main element here is the Concert Hall, at right angles to the Pump Room so that one end faces Abbey Churchyard. This hall of the 1890's was not wholly sympathetic to Baldwin and Palmer's work. For its idiom, within and without, was imitation Palladian, and so closer to Wood the elder than to the more restrained classicism of 1796. Anachronistic touches appear also in Brydon's extensions which flank Baldwin's Guildhall. They are the earliest of his works in Bath. Though their exterior is mostly Adamesque like the older building, each wing is capped by a pleasant little *cupoletto* much closer in spirit to the Baroque of Wren (plate 26). Round the corner in Bridge Street, Brydon was less constrained by

45 RIVERSIDE VISTA, Brunel.
Baroque.

46. OLDFIELD PARK; ST. ALPHEGE, by Sir Giles Gilbert Scott.

47. SNOW HILL;
The Point Block.

48. LYNCOMBE COACH HOUSE.

existing buildings in his Art Gallery cum Library which commemorated Victoria's Diamond Jubilee. Though he included some Palladian references, the domed corner composition, and the Library entrance with its ornately canopied niche to contain the Queen's statue, are admirable late nineteenth-century Baroque. Brydon's work as a whole is immensely preferable to the neo-Jacobean bulk of the Empire Hotel, as bad in this central setting as a gasometer could have been, which closed the century.

One need linger only briefly over the domestic buildings of a much expanding city. The dictum that Bath was England's Florence had caused the building, up Bathwick Hill, of some entrancingly sited Italianate villas with Italian names; throughout the century Italianate idioms were continued in separate houses up Lansdown, along Newbridge Hill, and elsewhere. Earlier on, a few Gothic houses had impinged on Bath's prevalent manner, and in Prior Park Road some Oxford-minded person built the picturesque pair of villas, with good Tudor chimneys, named Balliol House and Oriel House. The first is dated 1843; the latter is now a canine beauty parlour! Bath's dominant building practices were also, in these days before enforced insistence on local stone, infringed by the use of some other building materials. For some houses and streets in the district traversed by the Upper Bristol Road are largely of Bristol pennant or, as one sees in Hungerford Road which recalls the drabber areas of central or eastern Bristol, of pennant in front and un-Bathonian brick at the back.

Of Bath's Edwardian phase there is little to say. The social scene was still that of staid residents, and of opulent visitors ensconced and cossetted amid the potted palms of large, luxurious hotels. It was still the time for lapdogs and ladies' maids, of mainly horse-drawn, to our eyes unbelievably scanty traffic, of elderly valetudinarians drawn silently along Bath's few level streets in ungainly, yet pleasingly "period" Bath chairs which had long superseded the Georgian sedans. New building, at all events in the much visited central area, had almost wholly ceased, for Bath was replete with manifold creations in her native stone. Only in Walcot Street have I spotted a small Edwardian building worth a pause— St. Michael's Church House, *art nouveau* with just a touch of neo-Baroque.

Chapter IX

THE MODERN PICTURE

JUST after the first World War there was much in Bath's social scene to recall the secure, expansive years. Residents remained much as they had been. So too did many of the visitors, for the four large hotels were still open for long, leisured, luxurious sojourns by those seeking renewed health in an atmosphere little troubled by the humbler doings of a changed world outside. So Bath's "accepted" character remained. Yet the city's life, for many permanent inhabitants, was much modified by an ever increasing flow of motor traffic, by growing industries, and by a greater rate of economic coming and going between Bath and Bristol. Many Bathonians worked in Bristol's more numerous offices or factories. Bristol businessmen were apt to find congenial homes in Bath, and some Bristolians earned their living by work in the neighbouring city.

Bath's buildings of the 1920's and 1930's are of only moderate note. More truly significant were some measures taken to preserve and maintain inviolate the city's Georgian heritage. A wider appreciation of eighteenth-century architecture was now the accepted mode. But for many preservationists a Georgian building was still hardly old enough to deserve the zeal expended on something Norman or mediaeval Gothic. So Bath was ahead of its time when in 1925 and 1937 Local Acts were passed which took steps to control the designs of new buildings and the alteration of those already standing.

The Act of 1937, in advance of post-war legislation on such topics, provided for the listing of buildings earlier than 1820 thought worthy of protection from unworthy additions, or from such mutilations as the throwing out of unmannerly bow windows, the cutting through of cornices and stringcourses, and the violation of such balustrades as had not already fallen victim to the creation of attic flats.

New buildings, in a city where Bath stone was now universal for exteriors, and where neo-Georgianism in any case seemed fitting, conformed very largely to the fashionable trend. Such, without imitating actual buildings in Bath, were the Tuscan Electricity offices and the Corinthian Forum cinema not far away. The Co-operative Society built a pedimented block whose style clearly reproduced that of the Adamesque Westgate Buildings (so scornfully maligned by Sir Walter Elliot in "Persuasion") on whose site it was put up. Messrs. Colmer's shop in Union Street was given a frontage whose details imitated its late Georgian neighbours. A better building, well sited on a corner and the best neo-Georgian essay in Bath, was the new Post Office, well adorned, at its narrow end, with a Venetian window and a rounded Roman Doric porch whose style and details combine Gibbs's work at St. Mary le Strand and his Roman prototype in the church of Sta. Maria della Pace. Another Roman exemplar, Romanesque not Baroque, was used by Sir Giles Gilbert Scott for the Roman Catholic Church of St. Alphege which was started, in 1929, in Oldfield Park. For the building, with its cylindrical pillars, simple rounded arches, and carved capitals, and with a baldachino modelled on that in S. Clemente, is a most sensitive essay in the basilican manner which gave Rome so many of its earlier churches; the campanile, unfortunately, was never built to overtop the adjacent Somerset and Dorset Railway.

49.   LANDSCAPED CAMPUS; the University from the South.

50.   RIVERSIDE INDUSTRY; the Herman Miller factory.

The coming of war meant the immediate arrival of large sections of the Admiralty. It was a swift rush, bringing social upheaval, and a drastic change in Bath's economy which has persisted with the post-war continuance of Admiralty departments in the city, and is now admitted to be essential for its prosperity. Not all Bathonians, in those unhurried days of what was never, for the Navy, a "phoney" war, took the invasion to their hearts, and it was long before some of the newcomers attuned themselves to dwelling in a town so unlike London's suburbia. Bath's own human picture was subtly, drastically changed, and uniformed naval officers paced her streets as they had not done since the days of Nelson and Captain Wentworth. The large hotels and other buildings were taken over, with more requisitionings as war work increased and as the bombing of 1942 made some of the earlier offices unusable. New expanses of hutment offices (now housing most Admiralty departments still in Bath) were built on the city's upland outskirts. But the raids, despite Bath's attractions as a naval target, were in the "Baedeker" series which also ravaged Canterbury, Exeter and York. The casualties were heavy. The damage, though not in the shopping districts, was scattered and severe. St. James's church was gutted, as also were the Assembly Rooms. The Paragon, Norfolk Crescent, and Queen Square suffered fairly badly. Green Park and the Holloway district were seriously hit. But "area devastation", of the type which was serious in Bristol and still worse in Plymouth or Hull, was only seen along Julian Road and in the district between the Midland Station and Kingsmead Square.

Since the war Bath has not gone back to its peacetime pattern of life. The Admiralty departments have stayed and settled. The large hotels, with one short-lived exception, never opened again to receive their flow of wealthy guests. Industry, and work in Bristol, are still important for Bathonians. The city, very fittingly though only after some "teething troubles", has become a centre for Festivals of Music and the Arts; the main musical events, after varied early experiments, have been geared to the architectural fact that Bath has no *large* auditoria really suitable for occasions of Festival quality. Building activity has been in two main directions. Gaps and guttings have been made good in such famous spots as Queen Square, the Circus, Royal Crescent, and Somerset Place, while the Assembly Rooms have been carefully restored in the idiom of Wood the Younger's time. Many terrace houses have been converted into modern flats, in some cases by running two or more adjacent houses into single blocks.

New building, at first, was much as in other towns. Spread-out schools and council houses formed a high proportion of the whole, and as Bath stone facing was universal their exterior treatment was apt to have less colour variety and interest than one finds in similar buildings in some other towns. The houses, as at Foxhill and elsewhere, are occasionally pleasant modern essays in the terrace tradition inherited from the Georgians. Blocks of flats have also appeared. The most notable of such groupings, with Bath's one "point block" rising high among the well designed flat blocks of humbler elevation, is the Snow Hill development which replaces some Georgian slums, and has so given new life and seemliness to a steeply sloping area just North of the London road (plate 47). Individual houses have also sprung up, not always very happily for the townscape of Bath's outskirts, in several residential districts. In the still seclusion of Lyncombe Vale a "contemporary" house of much interest has been created by the complete transformation of what was once a coach house. The living room has been so cantilevered over the original

entrance as to command a charming diagonal vista along
the road, while the outside of that room is faced, in a
manner rare in Bath, with slates from the old roof
(plate 48).* New shops have also been built, in some
outer districts of the city, to serve those who inhabit new
or enlarged districts of housing; piazzas or terraces of
this type are seen, for example, at Weston, Twerton,
and (best of all) near the new houses at Foxhill. More
public architecture appeared, at various dates in the
1950's, in some churches built for different denominations. None, however, can be classed as buildings of much
novelty or outstanding distinction. The best, perhaps,
is St. Barnabas', South Down, a triple-cube building by
Mr. F. W. Beresford Smith, divided into eight bays by
concrete frames which are held to be logical successors of
the transverse stone arches of Gothic vaults. At Foxhill,
by way of contrast, the chancel arch of Mr. Alan Crozier
Cole's "Church Centre" is a curious "pavilion tower" in
a strongly Palladian idiom. More striking, completed in
1961 and superbly sited at the far end of Haycombe
Cemetery is the new, "contemporary" crematorium. It
has been well designed for this exquisite position, with
its entrancing view over the fields and trees of the valley
below, by the Corporation's Planning Department.
These southern uplands are inevitably important for the
current development of Bath. So it is here, on a lofty site
whence one can see the heights of Clifton, that an important new shoe factory has just been built by Messrs.
Clark of Street; monochrome monotony has here been
well avoided by using cladding panels of bright yellow
and blue.

Yet the central districts are those where this century's
contributions to Bath's townscape will mainly be seen.
An important new building is the block of shops and

* *See* also the *Journal* of the Bristol and Somerset Society of Architecst,
September, 1957, pp. 10–16.

flats on the site of the Grand Pump Room Hotel. One side had rightly to include part of Baldwin's curving *glorieta* at Bath Street's eastern end, so here was a reasonable case for neo-Georgian treatment. The new building, artistically less robust than its palatial forbear, has an Ionic colonnade to answer Baldwin's across Stall Street, while the sculpture above its main windows copies that of the same designer's work in Bath Street. Less restricted in their style are various buildings erected, or being built, elsewhere in the lower districts of old Bath North of the Avon. Close to Brunel's railway station the new Bus Station is an important building, good in its design but less so in parts of its finish. More important, for work of our own time, and mainly described in the next chapter, are the riverside below the site of Old Bridge and the Kingsmead district first developed by Strahan of Bristol.

Between Kingsmead Square and the Midland station various new buildings have already filled much of the ground cleared by wartime devastation. They include flats, shops, and office block (see page 117) and a new telephone exchange. Across from the disused station a southward road section includes a new Salvation Army Citadel, of effective contemporary design, offices for the Avon River Board, and a hostel and flats for old people whose appearance enhances this part of Bath's townscape. More disappointing, despite the eminence of Sir Frederick Gibberd its designer, was the first block of the new Technical College. For the fenestration, on one side of its gaunt rectangular structure, seems messy and disturbing, while pale grey panels below some windows, and the slabby expanse of its narrow wall, reveal the colour limitations of unrelieved Bath stone. Down by the Avon the ring road sweeps on, towards what was once the Quay, in a riverside drive which would be charming were it not for its view, over the river, of corrugated iron expanses and other graceless industrial features. We come, at last, to the single span which now makes up the crossing place of Churchill Bridge, a useful replacement, a little downstream, of the Old Bridge but less elegant than the fine single-arched bridges created elsewhere, over a century ago, by Goodridge and Tierney Clark.

Chapter X

MORE RECENT TIMES

SINCE 1961 the main events in Bath's history have
been more remarkable than the new buildings completed in its central area. Only after 1970 was important
progress made, in Southgate Street, in the area north of
the Quay, and up river from the Pulteney Bridge, on
buildings which are bound, whatever may be thought
about their architectural quality, to remain prominent
in the city's townscape.

With its population still about 85,000 Bath has
remained little more populous than it was in the early
1960s, with no sharp increases from London's "overspill"
or from major industrial developments. Its official
boundaries, since 1974 those of a District in the new
County of Avon, now include the whole of Combe
Down, an upland area above Weston village, and an
eastward extension, including Bailbrook House which
has now been restored, and given extra buildings, as
International Aeradio's Training College, almost as far
out as the village of Batheaston.

Despite a constant influx of new residents Bath's life
and prosperity are much conditioned by the occupations
of those whose actual work, as distinct from times of
holiday or retirement, is done in the city. It was therefore
important for Bath when, late in 1967, the Navy
Department decided to keep many of its employees in
the city. But a scheme to house them, in a single office

complex at Foxhill, on the Combe Down side of Bath has been cancelled for financial reasons.

Naval logistics apart, Bath remains a great regional shopping centre, and an important scene of such professional activities as education and hospital treatment, and of the catering found in its restaurants and in its fairly numerous, though not really large, hotels. Bath's industrial activity is also far from contemptible, and is much longer established than most of the light industry which has so greatly changed Cheltenham; industry thus contributes an element of much value, yet out of tune with the world-wide image of Bath as a gracious Georgian spa town and Festival centre. We shall see, however, that Bath's industrial establishments have of late done a fair amount to improve the city's architecture. Engineering of various kinds, including cranemaking by the famous concern of Stothert and Pitt, accounts for some five thousand workers. Printing and publishing, not all of it at Pitman's, employs nearly two thousand, while such goods as clothes and footwear find work for several hundreds. The making of furniture is another of Bath's industries.

Bath has now become a University city, with architectural results very apparent on Claverton Down. The status of a University town came to Bath not by the founding of a wholly new learned institution but by the gradual transfer of one already at work in Bristol.

What happened was that the Bristol College of Science and Technology, later elevated to full University rank, was temporarily housed, on Ashley Down, in blocks once used by the Müller Orphanages. Its authorities planned to move to Kingsweston, using the mansion by Vanbrugh as the nucleus round which they would build modern blocks. But the project was soon much expanded, and it became clear that the College would probably impinge disastrously on an attractive scenic area. The Bristol authorities refused planning permission for the large project with which they were then faced. In 1964 the College accepted Bath's offer to house the enlarged foundation, whose full University status came in 1966.

Like most of our wholly new Universities, with their great demand for space, that at Bath lies away from the city's historic centre, and from most residential districts. Its "contemporary" buildings will never excite neighbourly comparison with Georgian areas. Bath's University lies high on the windy plateau of Claverton Down. Part of the academic area is over six hundred feet up, and some ramparts of an Iron Age hill fort are within the northern confines of a University built to teach the technology of the Space Age. The site is that chosen, about 1839, for Queen's College, a public school whose buildings were started, but which never opened its doors to pupils.

A preliminary building, quadrangular in design and still existing, as the chemistry school, some distance from the main buildings of the campus, was erected by the CLASP method of industrial prefabrication. The main buildings, by the London architects Robert Matthew, Johnson-Marshall and Partners, are now virtually complete. The chief element in this mainly technological University is what one may call a linear campus. A road runs, through the campus and at ground level, from East to West. Above it, a central Parade is flanked and enclosed by academic and social buildings. The most central are the Library, with attractive and functional interiors, and the opposite block which contains the University Hall and the Senior Common Room. Varied cladding materials are used, in a more interesting way than at first seemed likely, on the exteriors of the different blocks, while a glazed footbridge links buildings which were opened back in 1968. At the Parade's eastern end the tall block of Norwood House, with the Students'

Union, a shop, and over two hundred study bedrooms, rises high to close the vista. More student accommodation, banks, more shops, and administrative offices are in Wessex House, another tall transverse block, now finished at the western end of the Parade; beyond it a mainly two-storeyed block contains the schools of pharmacy and pharmacology. Some blocks of student housing, in two differently arranged groups, lie away from the main buildings, while near the Library the small Chaplaincy Centre has pyramidal top lighting above its square chapel. South of the main University buildings one traverses a landscaped area whose main features are an artificial pond and a grassed and terraced open-air theatre. Rising above the whole site a slender multiple chimney emits the fumes of the heating system into the cool upland air.

While it was still the Education Authority the City of Bath remained active in the building of schools, the new fabric of the Diocesan Girls' School, below Fairfield Park, being larger and more imposing than most in this category. In the independent sector, two achievements deserve a mention. King Edward VI's School has moved its senior departments from Broad Street to a site in North Road whose chief building, a Victorian Italianate mansion, had already been a school. Extensive academic buildings, by the Bath architects Snailum and Le Fèvre, and including an Assembly Hall and teaching blocks, were opened in 1961. More notable, by the same architects and with its main feature a hexagonal multi-purpose hall, was a building finished in 1974. More recently, with Mrs. Pat Fereday as architect, a bursary, offices, a Governors' room, and sixth form group room have been included in a building which is largely the refacing and refashioning of a much older block.

Many changes have come to Bath's means of public transport. The one time Great Western Railway remains active and busy, but the Midland line from Mangotsfield and the Somerset and Dorset route have been closed. The Midland station, opened in 1870 with a fine classical forebuilding and an iron-arched trainshed like that of a miniature St. Pancras, is thus forlorn and disused. Several schemes have been bandied about for the future use of this building, and of the track area outside it, and for parts of the goods yard laid out by the Midland Railway just across the river. Suggested uses include those of a supermarket and a hotel, with car parking space provided in the trainshed or in part of the ground across the Avon. Two public enquiries have been held to decide the future of the station and its immediate surroundings, and the Minister for the Environment has now expressed his preference for a scheme including a supermarket and car parking.

The increase in Bath's vehicular traffic has also created unseemly strangulation in streets never meant for such a phenomenon. Various schemes for the handling of Bath's traffic have been tried out, and some lengths of street have been "pedestrianised". Now that Professor Buchanan's plan for the rerouting of some of central Bath's traffic through a deep cut and a short tunnel has fallen victim to financial restraints much of the city's heavier through traffic goes south of the river, along Claverton Street or the short new highway of Rossiter Road, and so along the Lower Bristol Road as it traverses the city's more industrial areas. Now, however, much heavy traffic that once flowed through Bath now uses the M.4 motorway, with easy access to M.5 and the central areas of Bristol.

Professor Buchanan also conducted a survey of Bath as a result of its choice as one of the "heritage" towns chosen by the Government for special survey as a prelude to a greater degree of conservation. The second Buchanan report on Bath came out in 1969. It specially noted the poor state of many buildings in the ancient centre, and the amount of unused space in the upper storeys of many such buildings. Since then Government money, local government contributions, and private finance have led to a great deal of renovation and repair work, and the ingenious reuse of many buildings; the main emphasis in central Bath is now on this work rather than on wholly new construction.

The cleaning and reconditioning of the facades in the Circus has now been finished, and the same subsidised process is now nearly complete in Pulteney Street. In that street and in Laura Place the most spectacular change is the gradual reconditioning of what was once the Pulteney Hotel. The building is being converted, by architects in Worthing, into a group of over sixty luxurious flats, to be called Connaught Mansions from the frequent visits to the Pulteney Hotel of the Duke of Connaught. Original features, comparatively few but including some fireplaces, are being kept, as also are the opulent Edwardian classical interiors, including a domed and glazed winter garden, and the newly subdivided dining room with its rococo ceiling panels and its clusters of pink scagliola Ionic pillars, all by the local architects Silcock and Reay.

Not far away in Grove Street the Old Prison has been cleaned and restored outside, with its interior gutted and fitted out as modern flats. In the same street some other changes are less happy. Houses by the Bath architect John Eveleigh, with a late Georgian window uniquely dated 5792 instead of A.D. 1788, had become sadly derelict and have now been pulled down to make way for "period" replacements and more obviously modern buildings. The nearby Old Brewery has been fitted out, with a fair amount of new windows, as a group of flats. In the same area of Bath some important renovation work on the Pulteney Bridge, completed in 1976, has

partially restored it to the appearance it had when
Robert Adam's design had been rendered in the 1770s.

In the very middle of the historic city the Pump Room
and its adjoining buildings have been beautifully cleaned
and, where necessary, their stonework has been repaired;
the late eighteenth-century building now has the
splendour and beauty that such visitors as Nelson and
Jane Austen would have admired. Across the Abbey
churchyard the northern half of the house once that of
Marshall Wade, pre-Palladian of the early eighteenth-
century with important changes made about 1830, has
been restored and, more recently, cleaned outside. It
now belongs to the Landmark Trust, with the National
Trust using its lower storeys as a shop. Close at hand
Ralph Allen's town house, with its view towards Bathwick Hill still nearly blocked, has been renovated as
offices, with cleaning and restoration done on the somewhat narrow central portion of its eastern facade.

Restoration work done, in Abbey Green, by the Bath
Preservation Trust has been followed, at the green's
south-western corner, by the building, in a Georgian
idiom, of the enclosing block of St. Michael's arch*,
with two storeys of flats above it. The conservation
scheme in Old Orchard Street and Pierrepont Place has
been finished, and more renovation has improved
North Parade Buildings, where the one-time Salvation
Army hostel, with some "period" features surviving
amid much former desolation and little shops made to
lead off the back area, has become a set of flats known
as Hamilton House.

In Bath's main shopping area work has started,
after controversy and with a replica frontage due to
replace the curve of the older buildings from just before
1800, of the block (long known as the Plummer Roddis

*The name comes from the trade name used by Marks and Spencer's, who
contributed to the cost.

block) on the southern side of New Bond Street. Up Broad Street the repair and cleaning of the Old Grammar School's facade is one of Bath's best achievements in the now widespread field of urban renovation.

Near the top of Broad Street the Knightstone Housing Association, which has done much work of this kind in Bath and Bristol, is now fitting out new flats in the first houses of Fountain Buildings. Several houses have been, or are being cleaned or refitted in the Paragon. Down between Walcot Street and the river two houses in Chatham Row have been restored, with the preservation of most of their good internal features. Another house is now under repair, and the abandonment of the Buchanan tunnel scheme should mean better hopes for the future of this down at heel domestic range.

On the lower slopes of Lansdown two historic buildings have had notable improvements. In Julian Road the eighteenth-century Riding School, once Christ Church's parish hall, is being reroofed and fitted out as a set of flats, houses, and maisonettes. Further up the hill the Real Tennis Court of the 1770s has found a much subdivided new use as the Camden Works Museum of workshop survivals and engineering technology; it well complements the excellent carriage museum now installed in Circus Mews.

In Beaufort Square renovation and conversion work, long overdue, is soon to start on the houses, of the 1730s, along the northern side. But the northern frontage of the Theatre Royal, now owned by a Trust whose Chairman is Mr. Jeremy Fry, still awaits the cleaning and restoration it so much needs. One hopes that this work, which can attract Government aid, will be included in the costly improvements now projected.

In Kingsmead Square one of Bath's most spectacular feats of restoration, and of the cleaning and renewal of stonework, has been the renovation, for use as offices and flats, of the terrace range of the 1730s along the square's southern side. Many schemes for this range's future were discussed before the actual operations, which involved some new structural work at the back, were started. Not far away, at the far end of Westgate Buildings, the renovation of the last two houses was a delicate, complicated task, particularly with the near collapse of the back structure of a building which has now been made good.

West of Kingsmead Square the slow, house by house rehabilitation of New King Street has made steady progress. One hopes that work will soon start on the sadly decayed, picturesque little enclosure of St. Ann's Place. In Great Stanhope Street nothing has yet been done on the filling in, presumably with a mock Georgian frontage, of the long gap caused by the collapse of a whole row of houses. But round the corner from the far end of that street the late Georgian houses in the short highway of Nile Street have, after much delay, been restored as flats.

Thoughts on older buildings lead one to consider the sadly large number which the city has lost in the last fifteen years. Casualties have been high, though no one need much regret those pulled down to make way for the architecturally interesting but over-extensive shopping precinct now finished between Newark and Southgate Streets. South of the river the early eighteenth-century Cold Bath, and some pre-Georgian mullioned houses at the bottom of Holloway, sadly made way for part of the road widening along Claverton Street. The Lyncombe Poor House was replaced by modern housing, while a humble terrace of canal workers' cottages was pulled down on its site which overlooked the first reconditioned reach of the canal. But at the bottom of Prior Park Road the row of cottages put up by Ralph Allen to house workers on his tramway and on his nearby stone wharf has been saved from demolition after a public enquiry. Various schemes for the rehabilitation of the houses have been put forward; it remains to be seen which one of them is chosen. On Broad Quay some simple warehouses were replaced by a somewhat overpowering office block; the additional office block of Quay House has now been added behind it.

Behind the Royal Crescent the Victorian ruins of St. Andrew's church were cleared, and the site has been grassed over. A little to the East controversial demolitions led to some of Bath's most unattractive modern buildings. Humble, decayed, but still pleasing housing in Ballance and Morford Streets, on Lansdown Hill, and in the high-perched blind alley of High Street mostly disappeared to make way for blocks of Corporation flats, in their scale matching Portland Place and Burlington Street, but with an excessive effect and some harshly overpowering roof structures. But the surviving Georgian houses in Morford Street have now been reconditioned, with a playground piazza laid out at the back and the houses now entered from that side. At the bottom of the street a short row of new houses, in a sympathetic but definitely contemporary style, are among the more meritorious new buildings in any central part of the city.

Down by the Avon, and above the Pulteney Bridge a riverside site has been filled by a two-tier car park, partly surmounted by the slablike "contemporary" block of the Beaufort Hotel whose interiors are, however, less unappealing than its harshly unsympathetic exterior. The rest of the space above the car park at one time chosen as the site of Bath's new Law Courts has yet to be filled by any new building.

The Guildhall area contains one of Bath's worst replacements of agreeable but not outstanding old buildings. A pleasant group of early eighteenth-century fronts, with later shop windows, was swept away to clear the ground for the most unfortunate new building in the lower part of the city. Despite changes in its design suggested by the Royal Fine Arts Commission the "Harvey" blocks, of shops below offices, is a graceless, ill-fenestrated apparition, put up where most visitors and local people are likely to see it; no mellowing of its surface seems likely to modify its offence.

Another new building, in its architectural quality below the opportunity of its site, is the new Police Station in Manvers Street. Opposite it is the garage cum office block of Lewis House, in its window intervals respectful of Bath's basic traditions but too dominant in its attic storey.

The Kingsmead area, largely rebuilt since its bombing and with a new shop and office block behind Strahan's southerly terrace in Kingsmead Square, contains several official buildings. A tall, narrow, somewhat unimaginative block, called Kingsmead House, holds various Government offices. Three blocks of flats, arranged round a car park, are more effective in their grouping of architectural masses, their balconies, and their external use of local stone. One, corresponding to the official building, has nine storeys, while another has ground-floor shops. A new Telephone Exchange is well placed on a corner site. It is a more interesting building, and less baldly rectangular than its neighbour, and its height is not unmannerly in its relationship to other new buildings in Kingsmead. But its projecting upper storeys, clad in dark copper, jut somewhat aggressively towards Charles Street, and the finished building makes a dauntingly ponderous end to the eastward vista along New King Street. Not far away, additions have been made to the Technical College; as for the earlier work the architects are Sir Frederick Gibberd and Partners. Most of the new buildings lie between Avon and Milk Streets, but a hexagonal Assembly Hall, more sightly

51.   THE SOUTH SIDE, Kingsmead Square, as renovated in the 1970's.

52.   New Housing; on the Whitewells estate.

than the earlier projecting lecture room, is nearer to the original complex.

Many houses, individual or in terrace groups, and many rows or blocks of flats have gone up in Bath during recent years; some of the latest are sited well out on the city's outskirts. The areas where one may find privately built houses are too many to specify, but Beckford Court (just off Warminster Road) and three blocks of flats, known as Pitman Court, at Lambridge Mill are good examples of this infilling. In Portland Place a block of fifty study bedrooms, built for University students, is leased from its builders by the Students' Union. In Monmouth Place, and down Cumberland Row, St. Paul's Place is a block of new flats, with neo-Georgian references but also with a more modern feeling, which makes a considerable contribution to that part of Bath's townscape.

Municipal housing has tended to be built in fairly large groupings, though a small estate of two-storey houses, terraced and stepped on a hilly site, with doubly sloping roofs, heavy projecting doorheads, and pleasingly blended soft green colouring, is in Claremont Buildings beyond Claremont Place. Less agreeable, in the somewhat feverish variety of their grouping, and in the architectural treatment of their partially timbered top storeys, are the flats and houses, above Twerton, of Lansdown View. The single-slope roofing and overhanging top storeys of some blocks seem unsympathetic to the locality; the same harshly revealed visual disaster of single-slope roofing facing out from a hillside is unhappily prominent in some ranges of flats in the privately built precinct of Calton Gardens just below Beechen Cliff. Higher up in southern Bath, and near the Navy Department's Foxhill offices, the considerable Springfield estate, of terraced flats and rows of small houses, is less notable for the appearance of its buildings than for the splendour of the downhill view, across most of Bath, from part of Meare Road.

Of greater merit is some housing in the extreme North East of Bath, an area little known to visitors. The three parallel blocks of Midsummer Buildings rise above Fairfield Park, Solsbury Way is worth noting, while in upper Larkhall the new Whitewells estate has some unassuming, attractive groups (see plate 52), like those in Claremont Buildings and well set against a high background of Lansdown slopes. A fine background, of Solsbury Hill and the Swainswick valley, also lies behind the two-storeyed groups, with lightly coloured boarding to set off their facing of "reconstituted" Bath stone, which are nicely set round the Rosehill Recreation Ground. In Eldon Place, along the southern side of the same open space, some old people's dwellings are partly in two small blocks but mostly consist of a charming single-storey row which does modest deference to Bath's great terrace tradition.

Churches have not, since 1961, been a leading element in Bath's new architecture; both of those which I now mention serve Roman Catholic needs, and have been ordered inside in full sympathy with the liturgical decisions of the second Vatican Council. One, at Combe Down, was designed by Mr. Martin Fisher of Bath. It is square, but is arranged diamondwise inside, with its roof supported by a single steel joist rising high above a top-lit sanctuary. At Southdown St. Joseph's is by Mr. W. D. Proctor of Bristol. Almost as broad as it is long, and with clerestorey lighting for its central section, it has a somewhat chunky exterior which belies the genuine attraction of its well unified worshipping space. Some of its furnishings were specially made. Others, of Victorian dates, come from a demolished Anglican church in Bristol.

Meritorious both as a new building and as an exercise in conservation is the new block which fills most of the space between Barton Street and Beaufort Square. A house by Strahan, with a notably charming, somewhat vernacular Georgian frontage, still stood next to the Theatre. Its destruction was proposed, but the Bath Preservation Trust put forward other ideas, and a developer was found to carry them out. Ernest Tew of Bath made designs for what was actually done. The surviving house was rebuilt behind its Strahan frontage, while the gap left by the destruction of its neighbours was filled by flats whose frontage continues that of the reconstructed Strahan house. A more "contemporary" range, of shops and flats, has been built to face Barton Street. Close at hand, the northern side of Trim Street was lately modernised, as far as Trim Bridge, by a new office block, bulkier than what it replaced but broadly sympathetic to its setting; it was put up by the firm of C. H. Beazer, the local builders and developers who have been, and are, prolific in present-day Bath.

Tough controversy soon engulfed a scheme for a new office block on a sensitive central site. The Bath and Portland Stone Company wished to replace their offices, just South of the Abbey, by a "contemporary" building. Robert Matthew, Johnson-Marshall and Partners designed what would, had it been built, have been a better piece of modern architecture than any new office block in Bath. It would however, less than thirty feet from the Abbey's South transept, have been a sharply unsympathetic neighbour to that early Tudor Gothic church. After two votes in the City Council, and a considerable display of public opinion, a Ministry enquiry was held, and the decision went against the proposed building. The firm has now built an office block, of modest distinction, on a site in Manvers Street.

Another office building of some quality, in an area where no sympathy with "period" buildings needed to be considered, lies between the river and the Lower Bristol

Road. By Hugh Roberts it is soon to be sold by Stothert and Pitt's. On its main frontage the plainness of local stone has been relieved, below the windows, by bluish green panels of asbestos with a plastic finish. Lower down the Avon Bath's riverside zone contains some industrial architecture better than most of what has recently appeared in the city centre. One building, in Locksbrook Road and with much corrugated aluminium in its roofing and curtain walls, is that of the engineering firm of Horstmann Ltd. Across the Avon Bath Cabinetmakers added to their older premises. Their new factory, with clerestorey glazing, was given outer panels of faced asbestos. Its architects were Yorke, Rosenberg, and Mardall, and it was much praised when it was opened in 1967. It is now, after alterations, used by another furniture-making concern, the Herman Miller Company whose headquarters are in the State of Michigan in the U.S.A., and who have now chosen Bath as their manufacturing and distribution centre for Britain and much of western Europe. Across the Avon they have built a second factory which has won many awards, and more commissions for its architects, as one of the best modern industrial buildings in England. Well exploiting its riverside site, and by the London architects Farrell, Grimshaw, the factory has a structural framework of steel, and exterior surfaces of tinted glass combined with fibreglass panels of a deep cream colour giving the building a distinctive appearance reasonably sympathetic to Bath's prevalent stone. Lower down the river the Rotork Engineering Company have added to their older buildings. New offices, with their walling mainly of glass, stand on the factory's riverward side, while Leonard Manasseh designed the extension, with curtain walling of reconstituted Bath stone, a glazed and projecting top structure with an unusual silhouette, and two pyramidal skylights. A westward extension, by Farrell, Grimshaw and allowing for the flexible use of its internal space, has also been finished. Further to the West, near the end of Brassmill Lane, one has a new factory and office block built for the Horstmann Gauge and Metrology Works and the warehouses and other industrial buildings of a small trading estate.

Back in the city's central area the Sports and Leisure Centre is an important new building, modern in its style and equipped with such facilities as squash courts and a large swimming pool, a large sports hall, sauna baths, a solarium, and a "fitness conditioning room". Its main disadvantage, arising from the hard fact that the exceedingly unattractive Pavilion was left standing, is its undue spatial and visual intrusion into the green expanse of the Recreation ground.

Below the Pulteney Bridge the realignment of the historic abbey weir, and the refashioning of the site of its mill, have been finished to Mr. Neville Conder's designs; they are part of a wider scheme for easing the Avon's floods. A new weir, whose shape, for aesthetic reasons, is not unlike that of a boomerang, has replaced the "foaming diagonal" which long spanned the river. On the site of the mill, grass, trees, and a garden have been planted and a platform spans the millrace. A slipway, and two ramps for ascending fish, keep company with better landscaping and the much improved treatment of what was once a patch of unworthy desolation and neglect.

A SHORT BOOKLIST

The literature of Bath is very extensive, and I can only mention a fraction of it here. I have therefore, for the most part, confined myself to books of general importance for the history and architecture of the city. I have also listed certain authorities on which I have drawn during the writing of this book.

Rev. Richard Warner; *The History of Bath*, 1801.

Rev. Richard Collinson; *History of Somerset*, Vol. I, 1791.

John Britton; *The History and Antiquities of Bath Abbey Church*, 1825. Also the edition of 1887 as continued and supplemented by R. E. M. Peach.

Victoria County History of Somerset; Vol. I, 1906; Vol. II, 1911 (especially F. J. Haverfield on Roman Bath and the sections on religious houses, schools, and economic and social history).

John Wood the Elder; *An Essay Towards the Description of Bath*, 2 vols., 1742 and later edns.

Mowbray Green; *The Eighteenth-Century Architecture of Bath*, 1904. This, however, is now largely superseded by:—

W. R. Ison; *The Georgian Buildings of Bath*, 1948, 1969; 2nd edition 1980.

R. E. M. Peach; *Street Lore of Bath*, 1893. Of some value, but to be used with considerable caution.

A Barbeau; *Life and Letters at Bath in the XVIIIth Century*, 1904.

Edith Sitwell; *Bath*, 1932 (a largely literary study; hardly anything on buildings).

R. A. L. Smith; *Bath*, 1944.

J. C. Trewin; *The Story of Bath*, 1951.

V. C. Chamberlain; *City of Bath*, 1951.

Willard Connely; *Beau Nash*, 1955.

H. M. Colvin; *Biographical Dictionary of English Architects*, 1660–1840, 1954, 1978 (for architects working in Bath).

N. Pevsner; *North Somerset and Bristol* (Penguin *Buildings of England* series), 1958.

Peter Coard; *Vanishing Bath*, 3 parts, 1970, 1972.

Barry Cunliffe; *Roman Bath Discovered*, 1971.

David Gadd; *Georgian Summer*, 1971.

Adrian Ball; *Yesterday in Bath*, 1972.

INDEX

Bridges, chapels, churches, hospitals, railways and stations, and streets are listed in separate sections. Illustration references are in heavy type.

Abbey (at one time cathedral); foundation of, 11-12; becomes cathedral, 14-15; church of, 11-12, 15-17, 18-23, 24-5, 26-7, 39-40, 43, 63, 84, 97, 118, **3, 4, 5**

Abbey Church House, 29, **6**

Abbey Churchyard, 36, 38, 98, 114, **41**

Abbey Green, 114

Abbey Weir, 122

Adam, Robert, architect, 59, 71, 114

Admiralty (now Navy Department), stay of in Bath, 103, 108-9

Aelfsige, abbot of Bath, 14

Alexander, George, architect, **95**

Alfred Buildings, 61

Allen, Ralph, 35, 37, 40, 42, 42n, 43, 47, 51-2, 56, 69, 114, 116

Alphege, St., 13

Anne, Queen, 31, 32, 53

Anne of Denmark, Queen, 29

Anstey, Christopher, poet, 63, 63n, 69

Armstrong, William, architect, **93**

Art Gallery and Library, 99

Assembly Rooms; Lindsey's, 47; Lower, 37, 89; Upper, 59-60, 60n, 62, 90, 103, 104, 115

Attwood, Thomas, builder, 61, 61n, 62, 68, 72, 76

Austen, Rev. George, 79

Austen, Jane, 1, 63; novels and characters of, 1, 63, 79, 81, 102, 103

Avon County, 108

Avon, river, 2, 3, 7, 11, 26, 40, 48, 63, 72, 74, 75, 82, 83, 89, 92, 106, 118-9, 120-1; navigation of, 44-5, 66, 94

Axford's Buildings, 61

Bailbrook, House, 108

Baldwin, Thomas, architect, 61n, 64, 68-70, 73, 76-7, **78**, 98, **106**

Bath: site of, 1-2; in Iron Age, 1-2; Roman occupation of, 3-7; Saxon conquest and occupation of, 8-13; Coronation at, 12; Norman occupation of, 13; burning of (1087), 14; Civic status, charters, etc., 17, 27; cloth trade in, 18, 26-7, 29, 30, 94; Corporation (and Mayor) of, 17, 27, 55; revival of spa in, 27, 29, 30, 60, 65; XVIIth century buildings in, 29; in Civil War, 29-30; in Monmouth Rebellion, 30-1; lack of social facilities in, 31; work of Beau Nash in, 32-5; importance of for English social history, 34-5; XVIIIth century popularity of, 36; comparison with New York, 36; in Jacobite Rising (1715-16), 38-41; physical expansion of, 42-3, 45, 57-9, 70-2, 72-7, 99; Palladian development of, 45-51; building contractors in, 60-2; roads round, 64-5, 92; becomes a "residential" town, 79; church and chapel building in, 84-7; small houses and villas in, 90-1; flats and individual houses in, 116; modern

industry in, 94-5, 101, 104, 105, 109, 121-2; Victorian classicism in, 95-6, 98-9; neo-Romanesque in, 96;, in Edwardian period, 99-100; between the wars, 101-2; Admiralty in, 103, 109; air raids on, 103; since second World War, 103-7, 108-23; population of, 13, 18, 81, 81n, 94, 108; traffic in, 112-14
Bath Acts, 1925 and 1937, 101-2
Bath Cabinet Makers, 122
Bath and Portland Stone Co., 121
Bath and West Society, 64-5
Bath Preservation Trust, 114, 121
Baths, the, 47, 59
Bathampton, road to, 90
Batheaston, 2, 64, 108
Bathwick, 48, 67, 70-2, 79, 91
Bathwick Hill, 82, 84, 90, 99, 116
Beaufort Hotel, 117
Beaufort Square, 53, 88, 115, 121, **12**
Beaufort, Henry Somerset, 2nd Duke of, 35, 39, 44
Beazer, C. H. & Co., 121
Beckford's Tower, 86, 96
Beechen Cliff, 1, 2, 17, 107, 119
Bellot, Thomas, 26-7
Belmont, 61-2
Beresford-Smith, F. W., architect, 105
Berkeley, James, 3rd Earl of, 40-1
Bird, William, prior of Bath, 19-20, 23
Bladud, legend of, 1, 57
Bladud's Buildings, 61
Blue Coat School, 37, **45**
Brewery, old, 113
BRIDGES: Churchill, 107; Cleveland, 92; New, 93; North Parade, 92; Old, 53, 106, 107; Pulteney, 71, 108, 113-14, 117, 123, **25**; Victoria Suspension, 92-3.
Bristol, 3n, 9, 14, 16, 17, 18, 20, 26, 30, 31, 38, 40, 42-3, 44-5, 48, 48n, 50, 52, 53-4, 56, 58, 59, 59n, 64, 65-6, 67, 85, 88, 93-4, 97, 99, 101, 103, 104, 106, 109, 110, 114
Bristol Hotwells, 36, 48n
Brunel, Isambard Kingdom, engineer, 94-5
Brydon, J. M., architect, 98-9
Buchanan, Prof. Sir Colin, 112-13, 122
Burghley, William Cecil, Baron, 26, 27
Bus Station, 106

Calton Gardens, 119
Cambridge, 3, 21, 22, 28, 38, 89, 90
Cambridge Place, 90
Camden, Charles Pratt, 1st Earl, 69, 75
Camden Crescent, 74-5, 91
Camden Place, 91
Campbell, Colen, architect, 45, **52**

Thayer, Humphrey, apothecary, 47
Theatre in Bath, 66
Theatre Royal, 88-9, 115, 121
Tierney Clark, engineer, 92, 107
Tours, John of, Bishop of Bath and Wells, 14-15
Trier (*Augusta Treverorum*), 5, 7
Tufnell, Samuel, sculptor, 43
Tunbridge Wells, 33, 35
Turnpike Trusts: Bath, 65-6, 65n, 92; Bristol 92,
Twerton, 2, 18, 29, 105, Cook's factory at, 94, 115

University, the, 109-11, 118, **49**
Upper Bristol Road, 99
Upper East Hayes, 90

Vertue, Robert and William, architects, 21-2
Victoria, Queen, 92-3, 99
Victoria Park, 93

Wade, Marshal George, 38, 41, 43, 69, 114
Walcot, 2, 27, 56; church, 67, 72, 87; Methodist church, 87
"Walcot New Town", 43, 48, 59-60, 62
Waller, Sir William, 30
Walpole, Horace, 47, 58, 64
Wells, 12, 14-15, 17, 31
Wells Road, 82
Wesley, John, 33
Westgate Buildings, 102, 116
Weston, 90, 94, 105, 108; church at, 84
Weymouth, 35
Whitewells Estate, 120, **52**
Widcombe Crescent, 82-3
Widcombe Hill, 90, 96
Widcombe Terrace, 82-3
Wilkins, William, architect, 89
William II, King, 14-15
William III, King, 31
William "of Worcester", topographer, 16, 23
Wilson, James, architect, 95-6
Wood, John, the elder, architect, 43-53 *pass*, 55-7, 58, 74n, 98
Wood, John, the younger, architect, 57-9, 60, 61-2, 64, 65-6, 68, 73, **104**
Worcester, 11, 15, 37
Wyndham, Sir William, 39, 41

York House Hotel, 64
Yorke, Rosenberg, and Mardall, architects, 122
Young, Arthur, agriculturalist, 65
Y.M.C.A. Building, 98